ALAN AYCKBOURN

Confusions

Notes and questions by Tim Bezant

HEINEMANN·METHUEN

Heinemann Educational,
a division of Heinemann Educational Books Ltd,
Halley Court, Jordan Hill, Oxford OX2 8EJ
OXFORD LONDON EDINBURGH
MADRID ATHENS BOLOGNA PARIS
MELBOURNE SYDNEY AUCKLAND SINGAPORE TOKYO
IBADAN NAIROBI HARARE GABORONE PORTSMOUTH NH (USA)

First published as an acting edition only by Samuel French Ltd, London in 1977
First published by Heinemann/Methuen 1989 in the *Hereford Plays* edition
First published in the *Heinemann Plays* series 1992

    94 95 96 97 11 10 9 8 7 6 5 4 3

A catalogue record for this book is available from the British Library on request.
ISBN 0 435 23300 9

Cover design by Keith Pointing
Designed by Jeffery White Creative Associates
Typeset by Taurus Graphics, Abingdon, Oxon
Printed by Clays Ltd, St Ives plc

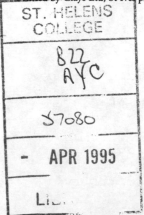

CONTENTS

Preface   v

Introduction   vii

Author's note   xiii

Cast details   xiv

Confusions

Mother Figure   1
Drinking Companion   19
Between Mouthfuls   39
Gosforth's Fête   61
A Talk in the Park   86

Activities and Explorations

1 Keeping Track: Mother Figure   95
                    Drinking Companion   96
                    Between Mouthfuls   97
                    Gosforth's Fête   97
                    A Talk in the Park   98
2 Explorations: A   Characters   99
                    B   Themes   102
                    C   In performance   102
                    D   Criticism   103

Bibliography   105

Appendix   107

PREFACE

In this edition of *Confusions*, you will find notes, questions and activities to help in studying the play in class, particularly at GCSE level.

The introduction provides background information on the author, the writing of the play, the circumstances of its various productions and advice on how to read and perform the play.

The activities at the end of the book range from straightforward *Keeping Track* questions which can be tackled at the end of each act to focus close attention on what is happening in the play, through to more detailed work on characters and themes in *Explorations*.

There is also a bibliography with details both of Alan Ayckbourn's other work and some recent works of criticism which might be useful reference sources for further study. There is also an appendix listing Alan Ayckbourn's major plays.

If you are already using the Hereford edition of *Confusions*, you will find that the page numbering in the actual playscript is the same, so allowing the two editions to be easily used side by side.

INTRODUCTION

Alan Ayckbourn

Alan Ayckbourn is one of the most prolific writers for the English stage, having written and produced, on average, one full-length play or comedy every year since 1965. Virtually all of his plays are first produced at the Stephen Joseph Theatre, Scarborough, where Ayckbourn is Director of Productions. The vast majority are then produced in London, where they enjoy considerable critical acclaim and public popularity.

As with his plays, Ayckbourn's own theatrical roots lie in Scarborough. After working as an Assistant Stage Manager with actor-manager Sir Donald Wolfit's company in 1956 (when he was 17), Ayckbourn joined the company based at the Library Theatre-in-the-Round in Scarborough led by Stephen Joseph. It was while Ayckbourn was acting with this company that Stephen Joseph encouraged him to write for production, and it was at the Library Theatre that his first plays (*The Square Cat* and *Love After All*, written under the pseudonym of 'Roland Allen') were produced in 1959, when Ayckbourn was twenty.

From Scarborough, Ayckbourn moved on to Stoke-on-Trent, where he helped to found the Victoria Theatre. Here he continued to act, direct and, most importantly, to write, and it was from the Victoria Theatre that *Mr Whatnot* received a London production in 1964, albeit unsuccessfully. On leaving the Victoria Theatre, he worked as a radio producer for the BBC in Leeds from 1965 to 1970, combining his work there with writing and directing at the Library Theatre. It was during this period that *Relatively Speaking* was written and produced in Scarborough: its successful production in London in 1967 marked Ayckbourn's permanent arrival upon the national stage.

His growing importance was consolidated in 1970 with the London production of the comedy *How the Other Half Loves*, which had been produced originally during the previous year in Scarborough. It was also in 1970 that Ayckbourn was appointed Director of Productions at the Library Theatre, in eventual succession to Stephen Joseph, who had died three years previously. From now on, Ayckbourn's career started to follow the pattern which it still follows today; within the constraints of his job as Director of Productions (which occupies the vast majority of his time), he has written a play per year for production at Scarborough which is then produced in London during the next two years. A full list of Ayckbourn's major plays and their dates of production will be found in the Appendix. *Confusions* is no exception to this pattern, being produced originally in Scarborough in 1974, then receiving its London production in 1976.

A brief survey of some of the plays produced during the years 1970 to 1986 gives a broad indication of Ayckbourn's content and themes, many of which are also found in *Confusions*. *Absurd Person Singular* is set in three married couples' kitchens over three successive Christmases. It charts the rise of the first couple in comparison to their social superiors: by the third Christmas, the original social positions appear to be reversed. In *Absent Friends*, a group of old friends attempt to comfort Colin, whose fiancée has recently died. Colin, however, is quite happy with his memories of her, and his happiness only serves to deepen the unhappiness of his would-be comforters in their own marriages and relationships. *Season's Greetings* portrays a family gathering at Christmas, and all the conflicts that such an event entails. Two sisters squabble over a guest, one at the possible expense of her already shaky marriage to a man who no longer pays her any real attention.

Way Upstream, set on a river cruiser (and staged on water

in Scarborough, London and Stoke), shows the effect of a strong-willed intruder on a weak-willed married couple who eventually survive the threat to their relationship and their lives. Finally, *A Small Family Business*, described by its author as a 'modern morality play', charts the compromises made by a businessman intent on honesty as he uncovers various levels of corruption within the family business. This eventually leads to murder and Mafia-like drug-dealing, while, ironically, unknown to him, his own daughter appears to be dying of her addiction. Ayckbourn's settings are nearly always those of the 'comfortable middle class' and are always instantly recognisable, as are his characters. Out of these apparently ordinary settings and characters, Ayckbourn creates situations that reveal the discomfort and pain lying beneath the surface of 'normality'.

The pattern of Ayckbourn's work outlined above continued until 1986, when he took a two-year break from his duties in Scarborough in order to run and direct a company at the National Theatre in London, where several of his plays (*Bedroom Farce, Sisterly Feelings, Way Upstream* and *A Chorus of Disapproval*) had already been produced. He directed four plays in two years and the success of his production of Arthur Miller's *A View From the Bridge* confirmed his status as a major director as well as a major playwright, earning him the 'Plays and Players' award for Best Director.

In 1988 Ayckbourn resumed his work in Scarborough, while continuing to write. His most recent plays are *Times of my Life* and *Wildest Dreams*. He has also just completed a musical called *Dreams from a Summer-house*. Doubtless, Ayckbourn is already at work on his next play.

Confusions

At present, apart from small-scale revues, *Confusions* is unique in Ayckbourn's body of work of full-length plays and comedies because it is a linked series of one-act plays designed to be played together under their collective title. As noted above, it was originally produced in Scarborough in 1974 at the Library Theatre-in-the-Round. When produced in London in 1976, it was seen at the proscenium arch Apollo Theatre. On each occasion, however, the twenty-two parts were played by just five actors and actresses. Not only was Ayckbourn experimenting with the one-act play, he was also experimenting with and challenging the abilities of his performers. The plays are linked by more than their title, for in each play (apart from the last, *A Talk in the Park*) one character forms a link with the next: Harry Compton leads us from *Mother Figure* into *Drinking Companion*, for example. These linking characters serve to provide some structure to the plays beyond their individual limits: as the characters of each play and the chain of events in which they are engaged are shown to be linked, however tenuously, so Ayckbourn creates a sense of a larger scale of events out of the smaller scale of the one-act play.

Style and Themes

As is usual in his plays, Ayckbourn takes an apparently normal or ordinary situation and setting and proceeds to play with it both in order to entertain and to draw his audience's attention to what concerns him most – and his concerns can be very serious indeed. That he chooses to treat them through the medium of comedy only serves to heighten the awfulness of what he reveals in the action of his plays, for while he keeps his audience laughing, they cannot help but be aware of the darker aspects of his plays.

Confusions is no exception to this rule. We may laugh, as indeed we are meant to, at Lucy in *Mother Figure* or Harry in *Drinking Companion*, but as we do so we are being made aware of, and are consequently appalled by, the circumstances which have brought them to their current situation.

Similarly, the device of hearing only what the waiter hears in *Between Mouthfuls* is, in itself, funny, but what he and we hear is the disintegration of two marriages. In *Gosforth's Fête*, just as anything that can go wrong in the preparations for the fête does so, the same occurs in the relationships between the people who are trying to put on the fête: hilariously, inevitably, the worst comes to the worst. Finally, *A Talk in the Park* is seen to be anything but a talk in the park for the characters involved.

In all five plays, we are invited to laugh at the characters and the situations in which they find themselves. As we do so, however, we cannot help but think whether we would do the same in that situation. We have to consider whether we are as at fault in our relationships with other people as Ayckbourn's characters are in theirs.

In Performance

Although these five one-act plays are intended to be played together to make up an evening's entertainment, that does not preclude the possibility of their being played or read separately. In a single evening's performance five separate sets would be necessary, designed so effectively that one could be removed and the next set up during, for example, Harry Compton's abortive telephone call home. It is worth considering how the various sets could be designed for maximum effectiveness for the audience's benefit as well as for ease of change-over during a performance as a means of adding detail to a reading of the play. Furthermore, it is worth considering what extra detail you would wish to add to the set for the audience's benefit over and above the bare detail provided in the stage directions. Finally, it is worth considering and visualising what costumes the various characters would wear to help establish the characters in the minds of the audience, especially if the same five actors and actresses were to play all the parts.

Reading the Play

It is important to read the individual plays aloud in order to appreciate what is left unsaid by the characters (and, hence, unwritten by the author) and to understand the changing interaction of the characters. It is only when Ayckbourn's characters are heard to speak for themselves that their depth, and consequently the writer's skill and understanding, may be fully appreciated. Care must also be taken with the stage directions, for frequently (and especially so in *Gosforth's Fête*) they contain detail an audience would take in visually which has a direct bearing on both the characters and the events in which they are engaged.

Because the individual plays are written for between three and five characters, they obviously lend themselves well to reading aloud in groups of this size. Read them aloud first of all to understand the action and the relationships and how they change: then explore and experiment with the text in order to discover more depth and understanding of the characters and why their relationships change.

Following the play text you will find two series of questions. Those in **Keeping Track** will help you to understand the action as it develops and may be worth using while reading the play for the first time. In **Explorations** there are more detailed and demanding questions organised according to *Character, Theme, Performance, and Criticism*. The questions in the latter section may lead into coursework assignments. All the questions are designed to stimulate knowledge, understanding and, hopefully, enjoyment of the play.

Tim Bezant

AUTHOR'S NOTE

These plays, although loosely linked, can of course be performed individually. When played together, it is recommended that they be presented in the order in which they appear here.

The entertainment was written originally for a cast of five (three male, two female). Obviously there are a wide variety of casting combinations which can be employed, depending on the actors available.

CAST DETAILS

First presented by Michael Codron at the Apollo Theatre, London, on May 19th, 1976, with the following cast of characters:

MOTHER FIGURE

Lucy	Pauline Collins
Rosemary	Sheila Gish
Terry	Derek Fowlds

DRINKING COMPANION

Harry	John Alderton
Paula	Pauline Collins
Bernice	Sheila Gish
Waiter	James Cossins

BETWEEN MOUTHFULS

Waiter	John Alderton
Pearce	James Cossins
Mrs Pearce	Sheila Gish
Martin	Derek Fowlds
Polly	Pauline Collins

GOSFORTH'S FÊTE

Mrs Pearce	Sheila Gish
Milly	Pauline Collins
Gosforth	John Alderton
Vicar	James Cossins
Stewart	Derek Fowlds

A TALK IN THE PARK

Arthur	John Alderton
Beryl	Pauline Collins

Charles	James Cossins
Doreen	Sheila Gish
Ernest	Derek Fowlds

The Plays directed by Alan Strachan
Settings by Alan Tagg

The action takes place in a living-room, a bar, a restaurant, a marquee and a park.

Time – the present

MOTHER FIGURE

LUCY*'s sitting-room. It is a suburban room, fairly untidy, with evidence of small children. There are two doors – one to the kitchen and back door, one to the bedrooms and front door.* LUCY *hurries in from the bedrooms on her way to the kitchen. She is untidy, unmade-up, in dressing-gown and slippers.*

LUCY *(calling behind her)*: Nicholas! Stay in your own bed and leave Sarah alone.

The telephone rings. LUCY *goes out to the kitchen, returning at once with a glass of water.*

LUCY All right, Jamie, darling. Mummy's coming with a dinkie . . . *(As she passes the telephone, she lifts the receiver off the rest and almost immediately replaces it.)* Mummy's coming, Jamie, Mummy's coming.

LUCY *goes off to the bedroom with the glass. The front door chimes sound. A pause, then they sound again.* LUCY *returns from the bedrooms.*

LUCY Sarah! You're a naughty, naughty girl. I told you not to play with Jamie's syrup. That's for Jamie's toothipegs . . .

The door chimes sound again. LUCY *ignores these and goes off to the kitchen. She returns almost at once with a toilet roll, hauling off handfuls of it as she goes to perform some giant mopping-up operation.*

LUCY Nicholas, if you're not in your bed by the time I come up, I shall smack your botty.

There are two rings on the back door bell. LUCY *goes off to the bedroom. A pause then* ROSEMARY, *a rather frail, mousey-looking woman, comes in from the kitchen.*

ROSEMARY (*calling timidly*): Woo-hoo!

LUCY *returns from the bedroom.*

LUCY (*calling as before*): Now go to sleep. At once. (*Seeing* ROSEMARY) Oh.

ROSEMARY Hallo. I thought you must be in.

LUCY (*puzzled*): Hallo?

ROSEMARY Thought you were in.

LUCY Yes.

ROSEMARY Hallo.

LUCY Hallo. (*A slight pause*) Who are you?

ROSEMARY Next door.

LUCY What?

ROSEMARY From next door. Mrs Oates. Rosemary. Do you remember?

LUCY (*vaguely*): Oh, yes. Hallo.

ROSEMARY Hallo. I did ring both bells but nobody seemed . . .

LUCY No. I don't take much notice of bells.

ROSEMARY Oh.

LUCY I've rather got my hands full.

ROSEMARY Oh yes. With the children, you mean? How are they?

LUCY Fine.

ROSEMARY All well?

LUCY Yes.

ROSEMARY Good. It's three you've got, isn't it?

LUCY Yes.

ROSEMARY	Still, I expect it's time well spent.
LUCY	I haven't much option.
ROSEMARY	No.
LUCY	Well.
rOSEMARY	Oh, don't let me – if you want to get on . . .
LUCY	No.
ROSEMARY	I mean, if you were going to bed.
LUCY	Bed?
ROSEMARY	(*indicating* LUCY *'s attire*) Well . . .
LUCY	Oh, no. I didn't get dressed today, that's all.
ROSEMARY	Oh, Not ill?
LUCY	No.
ROSEMARY	Oh.
LUCY	I just wasn't going anywhere.
ROSEMARY	Oh, well . . .
LUCY	I haven't been anywhere for weeks.
ROSEMARY	That's a shame.
LUCY	I don't think I've got dressed for weeks, either.
ROSEMARY	Ah. No, well, I must say we haven't seen you. Not that we've been looking but we haven't seen you.
LUCY	No. Do you want to sit down?
ROSEMARY	Oh, thank you. Just for a minute.
LUCY	If you can find somewhere. (*She moves the odd toy.*)
ROSEMARY	(*sitting*): Yes, we were wondering if you were alright, actually. My husband and I – Terry, that's my husband – he was remarking that we hadn't seen you for a bit.
LUCY	No.
ROSEMARY	We heard the children, of course. Not to complain of, mind you, but we heard them but we didn't see you.
LUCY	No. (*She picks up various toys during the following and puts them in the play-pen.*)

ROSEMARY	Or your husband.
LUCY	No.
ROSEMARY	But then I said to Terry, if they need us they've only to ask. They know where we are. If they want to keep themselves to themselves, that's all right by us. I mean, that's why they put up that great big fence so they could keep themselves to themselves. And that's all right by us.
LUCY	Good.
ROSEMARY	And then ten minutes ago, we got this phone call.
LUCY	Phone call?
ROSEMARY	Yes. Terry answered it – that's my husband – and they say will you accept a transfer charge call from a public phone box in Middlesbrough and Terry says, hallo, that's funny, he says, who do we know in Middlesbrough and I said, not a soul and he says, well, that's funny, Terry says, well who is it? How do we know we know him? If we don't know him, we don't want to waste money talking to him but if we do, it might be an emergency and we won't sleep a wink. And the operator says, well suit yourself, take it or leave it, it's all the same to me. So we took it and it was your husband.
LUCY	Harry?
ROSEMARY	Harry, yes. Mr Compton.
LUCY	What did he want?
ROSEMARY	Well – you. He was worried. He's been ringing you for days. He's had the line checked but there's been no reply.
LUCY	Oh.
ROSEMARY	Has it not been ringing?
LUCY	Possibly. I don't take much notice of bells. (*She goes to listen for the children.*)

ROSEMARY   Oh. Anyway, he sounded very worried. So I said I'd pop round and make sure. I took his number in case you wanted to . . .

   LUCY *is clearly not listening.*

ROSEMARY   Are you all right?

LUCY   Yes, I was listening for Nicholas.

ROSEMARY   Oh. That's the baby?

LUCY   No.

ROSEMARY   (*warmly*): Ah.

LUCY   I'm sorry. I'm being very rude. It's just I haven't – spoken to anyone for days. My husband isn't home much.

ROSEMARY   Oh, I quite understand. Would you like his number?

LUCY   What?

ROSEMARY   Your husband's telephone number in Middlesbrough. Would you like it? He said he'd hang on. It's from a hotel.

LUCY   No.

ROSEMARY   Oh.

LUCY   Whatever he has to say to me, he can say to my face or not at all.

ROSEMARY   Ah. (*Laying a slip of paper gingerly on the coffee-table*) Well, it's there.

LUCY   Would you care for a drink or something?

ROSEMARY   A drink? Oh – well – what's the time? Well – I don't know if I should. Half past – oh yes, well – why not? Yes, please. Why not? A little one.

LUCY   Orange or lemon?

ROSEMARY   I beg your pardon?

LUCY   Orange juice or lemon juice? Or you can have milk.

ROSEMARY   Oh, I see. I thought you meant . . .

LUCY Come on. Orange or lemon? I'm waiting.

ROSEMARY Is there a possibility of some coffee?

LUCY No.

ROSEMARY Oh.

LUCY It'll keep you awake. I'll get you an orange, it's better for you.

ROSEMARY Oh . . .

LUCY (*as she goes*): Sit still. Don't run around. I won't be a minute.

LUCY *goes out into the kitchen.* ROSEMARY *sits nervously. She rises after a second, looks guiltily towards the kitchen and sits again. The door chimes sound.* ROSEMARY *looks towards the kitchen. There is no sign of* LUCY. *The door chimes sound again.* ROSEMARY *gets up hesitantly.*

ROSEMARY (*calling*) Mrs – er . . .

LUCY (*off, in the kitchen*): Wait, wait, wait! I'm coming . . .

The door chimes sound again. ROSEMARY *runs off to the front door.* LUCY *returns from the kitchen with a glass of orange juice.*

LUCY Here we are Rosemary, I . . . (*She looks round the empty room, annoyed. Calling*) Rosemary! It's on the table.

LUCY *puts the orange juice on the coffee-table and goes out to the kitchen again.* ROSEMARY *returns from the hall with* TERRY, *a rather pudgy man in shirt sleeves.*

ROSEMARY (*sotto voce*): Come in a minute.

TERRY I'm watching the telly.

ROSEMARY Just for a minute.

TERRY I wondered where you'd got to. I mean, all you had to do was give her the number . . .

ROSEMARY I want you to meet her. See what you think. I don't think she's well.

TERRY How do you mean?

ROSEMARY She just seems . . .

TERRY Is she ill?

ROSEMARY I don't know . . .

TERRY Well, either she's ill or she isn't.

ROSEMARY Ssh.

LUCY returns from the kitchen with a plate of biscuits.

LUCY Here we are. (*Seeing* TERRY) Oh.

TERRY Evening.

LUCY Hallo.

ROSEMARY My husband.

LUCY Terry, isn't it?

TERRY Yes.

LUCY That's a nice name, isn't it? (*Pointing to the sofa*) Sit down there then. Have you got your orange juice, Rosemary?

TERRY sits.

ROSEMARY Yes, thank you. (*She picks up the glass of orange juice and sits.*)

TERRY Orange juice?

ROSEMARY Yes.

TERRY What are you doing drinking that?

ROSEMARY I like orange juice.

LUCY Now, here's some very special choccy bics but you mustn't eat them all. I'm going to trust you. (*She starts tidying up again.*)

ROSEMARY (*still humouring her*): Lovely. (*She mouths "say something" to* TERRY.)

TERRY Yes. Well, how are you keeping then – er, sorry,

I'm forgetting. Lesley, isn't it?

LUCY Mrs Compton.

TERRY Yes. Mrs Compton. How are you?

LUCY I'm very well, thank you, Terry. Nice of you to ask.

TERRY And what about Har – Mr Compton?

LUCY Very well. When I last saw him. Rosemary dear, try not to make all that noise when you drink.

ROSEMARY Sorry.

TERRY Yes, we were saying that your husband's job obviously takes him round and about a lot.

LUCY Yes. (*She starts folding nappies.*)

TERRY Doesn't get home as much as he'd like, I expect.

LUCY I've no idea.

TERRY But then it takes all sorts. Take me, I'm home on the nose six o'clock every night. That's the way she wants it. Who am I . . .? (*Pause*) Yes I think I could quite envy your husband, sometimes. Getting about a bit. I mean, when you think about it, it's more natural. For a man. His natural way of life. Right back to the primitive. Woman stays in the cave, man the hunter goes off roving at will. Mind you, I think the idea originally was he went off hunting for food. Different sort of game these days, eh?

ROSEMARY (*hissing*): Terry!

TERRY Be after something quite different these days, eh? (*He nods and winks.*)

LUCY Now don't get silly, Terry.

TERRY What? Ah – beg your pardon.

A pause. TERRY *munches a biscuit.* ROSEMARY *sips her orange juice.*

ROSEMARY Very pleasant orange juice.

LUCY Full of vitamin C.

TERRY   No, I didn't want to give you the wrong impression there. But seriously, I was saying to Rosie here, you can't put a man in a cage. You try to do that, you've lost him. See my point?

LUCY   That can apply to women, too, surely?

ROSEMARY   Yes, quite right.

TERRY   What do you mean, quite right?

ROSEMARY   Well . . .

TERRY   You're happy enough at home, aren't you?

ROSEMARY   Yes, but – yes – but . . .

TERRY   Well then, that's what I'm saying. You're the woman, you're happy enough at home looking after that. I'm the man, I have to be out and about.

ROSEMARY   I don't know about that. You'd never go out at all unless I pushed you.

TERRY   What do you mean? I'm out all day.

ROSEMARY   Only because you have to be. You wouldn't be if you didn't have to be. When you don't, you come in, sit down, watch the television and go to bed.

TERRY   I have to relax.

ROSEMARY   You're always relaxing.

TERRY   Don't deny me relaxing.

ROSEMARY   I don't.

TERRY   Yes, you do, you just said . . .

LUCY   Now, don't quarrel. I won't have any quarrelling.

TERRY   Eh?

ROSEMARY   Sorry.

LUCY   Would you like an orange drink as well, Terry? Is that what it is?

TERRY   Er . . . Oh no – I don't go in for that sort of drink much, if you know what I mean (*He winks, then reaches for a biscuit*) I'll have another one of these though, if you don't mind?

LUCY Just a minute, how many have you had?

TERRY This is my second. It's only my second.

LUCY Well, that's all. No more after that. I'll get you some milk. You better have something that's good for you.

TERRY (*half rising*): Oh no – thank you, not milk, no.

LUCY (*going to the kitchen*): Wait there. (*Seeing* TERRY *has half risen*) And don't jump about while you're eating, Terry.

LUCY *goes out to the kitchen.*

TERRY You're right. She's odd.

ROSEMARY I said she was.

TERRY No wonder he's gone off.

ROSEMARY Perhaps that's why she's odd.

TERRY Why?

ROSEMARY Because he's gone off.

TERRY Rubbish. And we'll have less of that too, if you don't mind.

ROSEMARY What?

TERRY All this business about me never going out of the house.

ROSEMARY It's true.

TERRY It's not true and it makes me out to be some bloody idle loafer.

ROSEMARY All I said . . .

TERRY And even if it is true, you have no business saying it in front of other people.

ROSEMARY Oh, honestly, Terry, you're so touchy. I can't say a thing right these days, can I?

TERRY Very little. Now you come to mention it.

ROSEMARY Niggle, niggle, niggle. You keep on at me the whole time. I'm frightened to open my mouth these days. I don't know what's got into you lately. You're in a

filthy mood from the moment you get up till you
go to bed . . .

TERRY What are you talking about?

ROSEMARY Grumbling and moaning . . .

TERRY Oh, shut up.

ROSEMARY You're a misery to live with these days, you really
are.

TERRY I said, shut up.

ROSEMARY (*more quietly*): I wish to God you'd go off
somewhere sometimes, I really do.

TERRY Don't tempt me. I bloody feel like it occasionally, I
can tell you.

ROSEMARY (*tearfully*): Oh, lovely . . .

TERRY If you think I enjoy spending night after night
sitting looking at you . . . (*He throws the biscuit
down*) What am I eating these damn things for . . .
you're mistaken. (*Thirsty from the biscuits, he grabs
her orange juice and drains it in one.*)

ROSEMARY That's mine, do you mind. (*She rises and stamps
her foot.*)

TERRY Come on. Let's go. (*He jumps up.*)

ROSEMARY That was my orange juice when you've quite
finished.

LUCY *enters with a glass of milk.*

LUCY Now what are you doing jumping about?

ROSEMARY *sits.*

TERRY We've got to be going. I'm sorry.

LUCY Not till you've finished. Sit down.

TERRY Listen, I'm sorry we . . .

LUCY (*seeing* ROSEMARY *'s distraught state*): What's the
matter with Rosemary?

ROSEMARY (*sniffing*): Nothing . . .

TERRY   Nothing.

LUCY   What have you been doing to her?

TERRY   Nothing.

LUCY   Here's your milk.

TERRY   Thank you.

LUCY   You don't deserve it.

TERRY   I don't want it.

LUCY   Don't be tiresome.

TERRY   I hate the damned stuff.

LUCY   I'm not going to waste my breath arguing with you, Terry. It's entirely up to you if you don't want to be big and strong.

TERRY   Now, look . . .

LUCY   If you want to be a little weakling, that's up to you. Just don't come whining to me when all your nails and teeth fall out. Now then, Rosemary, let's see to you (*She puts down the milk and picks up the biscuits.*) Would you like a choccy biccy?

ROSEMARY   No, thank you.

LUCY   Come on, they're lovely choccy, look. Milk choccy . . .

ROSEMARY   No, honestly.

TERRY   Rosie, are you coming or not?

LUCY   Well, have a drink, then. Blow your nose and have a drink, that's a good girl. (*Seeing the glass.*) Oh, it's all gone. You've drunk that quickly, haven't you?

ROSEMARY   I didn't drink it. He did.

LUCY   What?

ROSEMARY   He drank it.

LUCY   Terry, did you drink her orange juice?

TERRY   Look, there's a programme I want to watch . . .

LUCY   Did you drink Rosemary's orange juice?

TERRY   Look, good night . . .

ROSEMARY   Yes, he did.

LUCY   Well, I think that's really mean.

ROSEMARY   He just takes anything he wants.

LUCY   Really mean.

ROSEMARY   Never thinks of asking.

TERRY   I'm going.

LUCY   Not before you've apologized to Rosemary.

TERRY   Good night.

   TERRY *goes out.*

LUCY   (*calling after him*): And don't you dare come back until you're ready to apologize. (*To* ROSEMARY) Never mind him. Let him go. He'll be back.

ROSEMARY   That's the way to talk to him.

LUCY   What?

ROSEMARY   That's the way he ought to be talked to more often.

LUCY   I'm sorry. I won't have that sort of behaviour. Not from anyone.

ROSEMARY   He'll sulk now. For days.

LUCY   Well, let him. It doesn't worry us, does it?

ROSEMARY   No. It's just sometimes – things get on top of you – and then he comes back at night – and he starts on at me and I . . . (*She cries.*) Oh dear – I'm so sorry – I didn't mean to . . .

LUCY   (*cooing*) Come on now. Come on . . .

ROSEMARY   I've never done this. I'm sorry . . .

LUCY   That's all right. There, there.

ROSEMARY   I'm sorry. (*She continues to weep.*)

LUCY   Look who's watching you.

ROSEMARY   Who?

LUCY   (*picking up a doll*): Mr Poddle. Mr Poddle's watching you. (*She holds up the doll.*) You don't want Mr Poddle to see you crying, do you? Do you?

ROSEMARY (*lamely*): No . . .

LUCY Do we, Mr Poddle? (*She shakes Mr Poddle's head.*)
No, he says, no. Stop crying, Rosie. (*She nods Mr
Poddle's head.*) Stop crying, Rosie. Yes – yes.

ROSEMARY *gives an embarrassed giggle.*

LUCY That's better. Was that a little laugh, Mr Poddle?
Was that a little laugh?

LUCY *wiggles Mr Poddle about, bringing him close
to* ROSEMARY's *face and taking him away again.*

LUCY Was that a little laugh? Was that a little laugh? Was
that a little laugh?

ROSEMARY *giggles uncontrollably.* TERRY *enters from
the hall and stands amazed.*

TERRY Er . . .

LUCY *and* ROSEMARY *become aware of him.*

TERRY Er – I've locked myself out.

LUCY Have you come back to apologize?

TERRY You got the key, Rosie?

ROSEMARY Yes.

TERRY Let's have it then.

LUCY Not until you apologize.

TERRY Look, I'm not apologizing to anyone. I just want
the key. To get back into my own house, if you
don't mind. Now, come on.

ROSEMARY (*producing the key from her bag*): Here.

LUCY Rosemary, don't you dare give it to him.

TERRY Eh?

ROSEMARY What?

LUCY Not until he apologizes.

TERRY Rosie, give me the key.

LUCY   No, Rosemary. I'll take it. Give it to me.

TERRY   Rosie.

LUCY   Rosemary.

ROSEMARY   (*torn*): Er . . .

LUCY   (*very fiercely*): Rosemary, will you give me that
key at once.

ROSEMARY *gives* LUCY *the key.* TERRY *regards* LUCY.

TERRY   Would you mind most awfully giving me the key
to my own front door?

LUCY   Certainly.

TERRY   Thank you so much.

LUCY   Just as soon as you've apologized to Rosemary.

TERRY   I've said, I'm not apologizing to anyone.

LUCY   Then you're not having the key.

TERRY   Now listen, I've got a day's work to do tomorrow.
I'm damned if I'm going to start playing games
with some frustrated nutter . . .

ROSEMARY   Terry . . .

LUCY   Take no notice of him, Rosemary, he's just
showing off.

TERRY   Are you going to give me that key or not?

LUCY   Not until you apologize.

TERRY   All right. I'll have to come and take it off you,
won't I?

LUCY   You try. You just dare try, my boy.

TERRY   All right. (*He moves towards* LUCY.)

ROSEMARY   Terry . . .

LUCY   Just you try and see what happens.

TERRY   (*halted by her tone; uncertainly*): I'm not joking.

LUCY   Neither am I.

TERRY   Look, I don't want to . . . just give me the key,
there's a good . . .

LUCY   Not until you apologize to Rosemary.

TERRY   Oh, for the love of . . . All right (*To* ROSEMARY)
Sorry.

LUCY   Say it nicely.

TERRY   I'm very sorry, Rosie. Now give us the key, for
God's sake.

LUCY   When you've drunk your milk. Sit down and drink
your milk.

TERRY   Oh, blimey . . . (*He sits.*)

LUCY   That's better.

TERRY   I hate milk.

LUCY   Drink it up.

> TERRY *scowls and picks up the glass.* ROSEMARY,
> *unseen by* LUCY, *sticks her tongue out at him.* TERRY
> *bangs down his glass and moves as if to hit her.*

LUCY   Terry!

TERRY   She stuck her tongue out at me.

LUCY   Sit still.

TERRY   But she . . .

LUCY   Sit!

> TERRY *sits scowling.* ROSEMARY *smirks at him smugly.*

LUCY   (*seeing her*): And don't do that, Rosemary. If the
wind changes, you'll get stuck like it. And sit up
straight and don't slouch.

> ROSEMARY *does so.*

TERRY   (*taking a sip of the milk*): This is horrible.

> *Silence. He takes another sip.*

TERRY   It's warm.

> *Silence. Another sip.*

TERRY   There's a football international on television, you
know.

LUCY   Not until you've drunk that up, there isn't. Come
on, Rosemary. Help Terry to drink it. "Georgie
Porgie Pudding and Pie, Kissed the girls and . . .?"

ROSEMARY   "Made them cry."

LUCY   Good.

ROSEMARY/LUCY (*speaking together*): "When the boys came out
to play, Georgie Porgie ran away."

TERRY   (*finishing his glass with a giant swallow*): All
gone. (*He wipes his mouth.*)

LUCY   Good boy.

TERRY   Can I have the key now, please?

LUCY   Here you are.

TERRY *goes to take it.*

LUCY   What do you say?

TERRY   Thank you.

LUCY   All right. Off you go, both of you.

ROSEMARY   (*kissing her on the cheek*): Night night.

LUCY   Night, night, dear. Night night, Terry.

TERRY   (*kissing* LUCY *likewise*): Night night.

LUCY   Sleep tight.

TERRY   Hope the bugs don't bite.

LUCY   Hold Rosemary's hand, Terry.

ROSEMARY *and* TERRY *hold hands.*

LUCY   See her home safely.

TERRY   Night.

ROSEMARY   Night.

LUCY   Night night.

TERRY *and* ROSEMARY *go off hand in hand.* LUCY
blows kisses.

LUCY   (*with a sigh*): Blooming kids. Honestly.

The telephone rings. LUCY, *as she passes it, picks it up and replaces it as before. As she does so, the Lights fade to a single spot in a call-box.* HARRY *is there, with the receiver in his hand.*

HARRY   Oh, blast, not again. Hallo – hallo – oh, damn and blast. (*He jiggles the receiver*) Operator? Operator? Hallo – hallo . . . Operator, there must be a fault on this line . . . The line I have been trying unsuccessfully to dial. . . . Yes – six-four-one-nine. I mean, this is quite unforgivable. This is the third time I have reported it and I am still quite unable to make contact with my wife . . . Yes, well, thank you for your sympathy. Let's try a little action, shall we? Because I'm going to take this to the top . . . Yes, top . . . What? . . . No T – for Toffee, O for Orange . . . Oh, forget it. (*He rings off*) Give me strength.

HARRY *moves out of the box. As he does so, the Lights come up to full, and the set has now changed to –*

DRINKING COMPANION

A three-star hotel bar. Discreet muzak is being played. PAULA, *a girl in her twenties, sits alone at a table, her coat and handbag beside her. On the table are her own vodka and tonic and an unfinished whisky and soda.* HARRY, *a man in his forties, returns and sits beside her.*

HARRY	Sorry, sorry about that. Not getting lonely, are you?
PAULA	No.
HARRY	After all that, would you believe it, couldn't get through. I get the ringing tone then it just cuts off like that. I think there's a fault on the line. Cheers. (*He drinks.*)
PAULA	Who were you trying to phone?
HARRY	(*evasively*): Oh, just – family. You know.
PAULA	Your wife?
HARRY	Yes . . .
PAULA	You're married?
HARRY	Yes.
PAULA	Have you got any children?
HARRY	Yes, yes . . . Can I get you another?
PAULA	Oh, well, just one more.
HARRY	(*calling*): Waiter. (*To* PAULA.) Same again, is it? Vodka and tonic?
PAULA	Lovely.
	The WAITER *appears.*
HARRY	Ah, Waiter. We want the same again, here, please. Vodka and tonic and scotch and soda.
WAITER	Right, sir. (*He turns to go.*)
HARRY	You'd better make them large ones.

PAULA Oh, well . . .

WAITER Large whisky, large vodka, sir.

The WAITER *goes.*

HARRY You were saying you were just up here for a couple of days.

PAULA That's right. We go back tomorrow.

HARRY Extraordinary, you know. I was walking through Mason's this morning on the ground floor, and I saw you two there, you and your friend – what's her name?

PAULA Bernice.

HARRY Bernice. Pretty name. Paula and Bernice – lovely names – and I thought to myself, hallo, they don't belong here. They look right out of place. Two lovely personalities like yours just don't go together with Mason's. No, I thought to myself – they're from London I wouldn't mind betting. Up for a visit. Promoting that – what was it you were selling?

PAULA Perfume.

HARRY And I said to myself, I wouldn't mind betting, Harry, that what's more those will be staying at the "Crown". And then it just so happens I look out of the door of the bar here and lo and behold – there you are, standing in the foyer.

PAULA Coincidence.

HARRY Not really. There's only one place to stay in this town. Well, you've got the "Wheatsheaf" or the "Black Horse" but they're not to be recommended, take it from me. When you're here, always plunk for the "Crown". How have your demonstrations been going? All right?

PAULA Oh, extremely well. We're just on this short promotion tour for their new brand, you see.

HARRY Is that the delicious fragrance I can smell even now?

PAULA   Oh yes, I think I've got some on.

HARRY   Very very nice. Very very nice indeed.

PAULA   It's proving very popular. It's exotic without being cloying and can be worn equally well day or night.

HARRY   You get commission on it, do you?

PAULA   Yes. They pay very well.

HARRY   Well, you need some inducement to come up here. What do you think of the place?

PAULA   It's all right, I suppose.

HARRY   Dreadful. Dead and alive place. Goes to bed at six o'clock at night, you know. No word of a lie. I've walked through the main street here, the main street mark you, at seven-thirty p.m. on a Saturday night and there has not been one single soul.

PAULA   Good gracious.

HARRY   Not one single soul. Empty. Deserted.

PAULA   You often here?

HARRY   Once every two months or so. Just for a sales check really. I mean, my firm doesn't treat this area very seriously. Consumer demand is negligible. Our only stockist is Mason's. We're fairly exclusive, you see. That's why I was in there today going over our sales with Mr Molyneux. He's their chief chap, you know. Not at all bad when you get to know him but I must say our sales were very disappointing.

PAULA   We sold a lot of perfume.

HARRY   Yes, well, you'd be alright with that. But our line, you see, well, I suppose you'd call us *haute couture* – high fashion anyway. Cut above the average. Not much call for it up here. Predominantly working class, you see. Very small market.

The muzak fades out.

PAULA   There's not many young people. We noticed that.

HARRY   No. There's not many girls, like, well, like yourself
          for instance. Now, you'd look very good in some
          of our stuff. Very good indeed.

PAULA   Really?

HARRY   Yes. (*Staring at her*) Orange. Tangerine shades.
          That's your colour.

PAULA   Is it?

HARRY   Definitely. You ought to go in for tangerine
          shades, take my tip. I'm good at that, you know. I
          can match a woman to her colour like that. Almost
          do it automatically these days.

PAULA   Really?

HARRY   You're what I call a modern girl, you see. You
          need modern shades, modern styling. Have you
          ever modelled by any chance?

PAULA   No, I don't think I've quite the . . .

HARRY   Oh, come on, come on. We don't always want
          them like sticks of celery, you know. Bit of shape
          never did a girl any harm. Some of our styles
          would really suit you.

          The WAITER *returns with the drinks.*

HARRY   Ah. Thank you. Vodka and tonic there.

WAITER   Thank you, sir. Thank you, madam.

HARRY   Could you charge it to Room two-four-nine, please?

WAITER   Two-four-nine. Very good, sir. (*He waits.*)

HARRY   Oh, just a second, just a second. (*Fumbling in his
          pocket and producing a handful of silver*) Here.

WAITER   Oh. That's very good of you, sir, thank you.

          The WAITER *leaves.*

HARRY	Cheers. No, put it this way. In my particular line I've got to be able to look at a woman and say yes, you'd look good in so and so. Straightaway.
PAULA	Yes, I can see that.
HARRY	The same with you. No difference. Straightaway.
PAULA	Yes.

A slight pause.

HARRY	You married, by any chance?
PAULA	No. Not likely.
HARRY	What, don't you fancy it?
PAULA	Not at the moment.
HARRY	Very sensible. Take my word. Steer clear.
PAULA	Don't let your wife hear you say that.
HARRY	Well, you know what I mean. Always envy what you haven't got, don't you.
PAULA	Oh yes?
HARRY	Freedom. I miss that. In the old days if I'd walked in here, say and I'd met someone attractive – like I'm meeting you for instance . . .
PAULA	(*laughing*): Me?
HARRY	No – joking apart – seriously – well, you know, you could just allow things to happen.
PAULA	What sort of things?
HARRY	Well, that depends on the girl, doesn't it?
PAULA	Oh, I see.
HARRY	Cheers. Got a boyfriend, have you?
PAULA	One or two.
HARRY	Bet you have.
PAULA	Nothing serious. Nobody special.
HARRY	Playing the field?
PAULA	More or less.
HARRY	Why not? At your age. What are you? Twenty-

one, I'd say at a guess.

PAULA Some hope.

HARRY What, younger than that?

PAULA Twenty-five.

HARRY Twenty-five? Get on with you. Thirty-seven.

PAULA Oh yes?

HARRY Thirty-seven. I don't look thirty-seven, do I?

PAULA No.

HARRY Not bad for thirty-seven. Ready for another one?

PAULA No. I've hardly started this.

HARRY No, in my opinion you young people today are doing the most sensible thing you can do. I mean, I know there's a lot of people of my generation that you could call narrow minded but I think it's just marvellous that a girl like you today, she can take her time, look around, get to know a few men for herself – you know, even sleep with them if she feels like it – and no hang-ups. Marvellous.

PAULA What makes you think I do that?

HARRY No, what I'm saying is . . .

PAULA I don't go sleeping around, you know.

HARRY No, that's not what I was saying. What I was saying . . .

PAULA I don't fancy doing that.

HARRY No, no, quite. But if you did happen to fancy it, there'd be nothing to stop you. That's what I was saying.

PAULA Possibly.

HARRY I mean, that's all I was saying. Cheers.

PAULA Where do you live, then?

HARRY Me? London. Well, just outside. Luton really.

PAULA Oh.

HARRY And you?

PAULA Shepherd's Bush.

HARRY Oh, really? I know Shepherd's Bush very well.

Very pleasant. Parts of it.

PAULA Yes, it is.

Pause.

HARRY No, to get back to our previous conversation. Look at it this way. We're two adult people. This is now, the present, today. We can sit here and talk about – well, whatever we care to talk about – let's say for the sake of argument – sex – without feeling embarrassed. Now I think that's a tremendous step forward. When you think of the past.

Pause.

HARRY I mean, I'm able to sit here, enjoy a drink in the middle of a public hotel, talking to a very, very attractive girl, if I may say so, and not feel in the least embarrassed. And she can do the same. You can do the same.

PAULA It's a nice hotel.

HARRY Not bad. Not marvellous, but not bad. Cheers.

Pause.

HARRY The bedrooms are good. Have you got a nice room?

PAULA Fine.

HARRY Single?

PAULA No. We've got a twin.

HARRY We?

PAULA Me and Bernice.

HARRY Oh yes. That's your friend?

PAULA Yes.

HARRY I've got a double. I mean, it's just me in there but

I've got a double. I can't bear small rooms, you
see. Well, the firm's paying so why not. Besides,
better to be prepared, isn't it?

PAULA   How do you mean?

HARRY   (*laughing*): No, it's a particularly nice room, two-
four-nine. Always try and book it when I'm here.
En suite bathroom, all the trimmings. Here, look –
(*he produces his room key*) – two-four-nine, you
see. Room two-four-nine. If you should come back
here again, take my tip, try and get two-four-nine. I
think it is the quietest room they've got. Not round
the front, you see, it's round the side.

PAULA   That's good.

HARRY   Where are you two, then?

PAULA   Eh?

HARRY   What number?

PAULA   Oh, do you know, I can't remember offhand.

HARRY   Well, I hope your friend does. Otherwise you'll be
wandering round all night, won't you? Probably
finish up in two-four-nine if I'm lucky. (*He laughs.*)
Cheers.

Pause.

HARRY   Tell you what, are you likely to be paying a return
visit any time?

PAULA   What, up here?

HARRY   Yes, you'll probably be coming back sometime,
won't you?

PAULA   Shouldn't think so.

HARRY   You never know. When they see how much
perfume you've sold, they'll probably send you
straight back here to sell some more.

PAULA   It's only a temporary job.

HARRY   Well, if they should by any chance, you're bound to want to stay here again, aren't you? Nowhere else.

PAULA   I shouldn't think we'll . . .

HARRY   Well, what I was going to say is, would you like to have a quick look at two-four-nine? See if it'd suit you. You know, just in case you do come back.

PAULA   Oh no.

HARRY   No, I mean just literally pop upstairs, stick your nose round the door, see what you think.

PAULA   No, I couldn't really . . .

HARRY   Hang on, hang on, even better. Do you know what I've got up there? I've just remembered, I've got a bottle of whisky. Do you like whisky?

PAULA   No, I hate it.

HARRY   Of course, what am I saying, you're a vodka girl, aren't you? Tell you what, even better, I'll have a word with this chap, get him to send us up a bottle of vodka. I'll drink the scotch, you drink the vodka, we'll have a party.

PAULA   No, honestly, it's very nice of you but I'd rather not.

HARRY   Well, I mean, suit yourself. I mean, nothing like that. We can go to your room if you'd rather.

PAULA   No, thank you very much all the same.

HARRY   Ah, well. Not to bother. Just thought you'd care to have a look. Ready for another one?

PAULA   No, honestly, you've been very kind but I really have to be . . . (*Breaking off as she sees someone in the saloon bar*) Oh, here she is. Bernice!

HARRY   Hallo, it's your friend, isn't it?

                BERNICE *enters. She is a few years older than* PAULA.

HARRY   Hallo there. (*He rises.*)

BERNICE   You said in the foyer.

PAULA   I'm sorry. I met this gentleman, you see. Bernice, this is – er, Harry, isn't it?

HARRY   Harry Compton, how do you do?

BERNICE (*without really taking him in*): How do you do? (*To* PAULA) You said you'd be in the foyer.

PAULA   Well, we're only sitting here just round the corner.

BERNICE I didn't see you just round the corner though, did I?

HARRY   Now, can I get you a drink, Bernice?

BERNICE Yes, I'll have a gin and tonic, thank you.

HARRY   Gin and tonic for Bernice. Another vodka for Paula.

PAULA   No, no.

HARRY   (*calling*): Waiter! Can I take your coat, Bernice?

BERNICE No, I'll keep it on, thank you. I've been out there half an hour, you know.

PAULA   I'm sorry.

BERNICE Well . . .

HARRY   Now, now, now. Mustn't quarrel, girls. Waiter.

BERNICE (*sitting*): My God, this place is a dump.

HARRY   (*sitting again by Paula*): Just what we were saying, wasn't it, Paula? After six o'clock, absolutely dead.

BERNICE And it was freezing in that shop, what's more.

HARRY   Yes, it's very bad that. I mean there's no excuse for that. Waiter! Where the hell's he gone to? Hang on, I'll get them myself, it's quicker. Just wait there, girls, I won't be a second. Bernice's thirsty, we can't have that.

         HARRY *goes off to the bar.*

BERNICE Who's your friend?

PAULA   Oh, you know. He was the one hanging around the counter this morning. The one with all the funny remarks.

BERNICE	Oh, yes, that's right. That's him. How did you finish up with him?
PAULA	Because you were late and he caught me standing there on my own in the foyer.
BERNICE	I was not late. What's he like?
PAULA	Well, you know . . .
BERNICE	Let's go then, shall we?
PAULA	He's buying us a drink now.
BERNICE	So? We don't want to get stuck with him, do we?
PAULA	Well, we might as well have the drink now.
BERNICE	Alright. Then we'll tell him we've got to get back to our hotel. Tell him you're expecting a phone call or something.
PAULA	That's no good. He think's we're staying here.
BERNICE	How did he come to think that?
PAULA	I don't know, he just did. If we tell him we're at the "Wheatsheaf" he'll only follow us there.
BERNICE	He won't. (*She produces a scent spray.*)
PAULA	He will.
BERNICE	Why should he?
PAULA	Because he's one of those. We've only been talking five minutes and he's been trying to get me up to his bedroom.
BERNICE	I don't know why you wanted to come to this place anyway. (*She sprays behind her ears.*)
PAULA	Well, Simon said it was good.
BERNICE	You should know better than to trust Simon. (*She sprays behind her knees.*)
	HARRY *returns with drinks.*
HARRY	Here we are then, girls. (*Handing them out.*) That's the gin, that's the vodka.
BERNICE	Oh, that's a very big one.

HARRY   Well. Saves jumping up and down, doesn't it? Now then. Finished your argument? Cheers.

PAULA   Cheers.

HARRY   Been out looking at the town, have you?

BERNICE   Beg your pardon?

HARRY   Saw you'd got your coat on. Thought you might have been out.

BERNICE   Oh, yes I went for a walk.

HARRY   Not much of a place for walks, is it?

BERNICE   No.

HARRY   Well, this is the life, isn't it? When I woke up this morning and I knew I was due to come over here, my heart sank I don't mind saying. Then what happens? I finish up with two beautiful girls for company. Just goes to show.

PAULA   Yes.

HARRY   Paula and I, we've been chatting away, haven't we, Paula?

PAULA   Yes.

HARRY   Right, now. Let's see how I do with Bernice, eh, Paula?

BERNICE   What?

HARRY   Now, looking at Bernice – I immediately think of blue. Am I right? You look good in blue, am I right?

BERNICE   Me?

HARRY   That's your best colour. Best for you, if you're interested, blue.

BERNICE   No, I never wear blue.

PAULA   You've got that blue trouser suit.

BERNICE   I never wear blue. I hate it.

HARRY   Well, I could be wrong. It has been known, but it's unusual. You have another look at yourself in blue. See if I'm not right. I'm not talking about royal blue, not a dark blue – more of a pale blue. We've got this dress at the moment, it's in this new material, man-made fibre with ten per cent wool – crease-resistant – it's literally a dress you can roll in a ball, jump on it if you like, give it a shake, put it on, good as new. Now this is a really beautiful blue. A sort of ice blue I suppose you'd call it. Knee length, not a long one. It's got a top rather like you've got on now and I'm not joking, looking at your colouring, Bernice, it would really set that off. Can you see that, Paula, Bernice in blue?

PAULA   Yes, nice.

HARRY   She'd look really fantastic. When I saw you this morning at the counter there in amongst all your bottles and perfumes and things, I thought straightaway, that is the girl who could really wear that dress.

BERNICE   I wouldn't be seen dead in blue.

HARRY   Ah well. Cheers. No, as I say, I never thought I'd be spending this evening with two gorgeous girls.

BERNICE   You never know your luck, do you.

HARRY   Quite right, Bernice, many a true word. Never know your luck. Well, how are we three going to spend this evening?

BERNICE   Well, we're . . .

HARRY   Now, now. Plenty of time. Enjoy your drink first, then we'll decide. The night is young, as they say. So are we. Well, in my case, young in heart. (*He laughs.*)

PAULA   I don't think we'll be wanting to do very much this evening, actually.

HARRY   All right, fair enough. Let's stay here then. Fine by me. Have a bite of dinner later.

BERNICE   Oh no.

HARRY   It's very good, the restaurant here, you know.

PAULA   Oh no.

HARRY   On me. On me, I don't often have the pleasure.

BERNICE   I don't think either of us are very hungry, thank you.

HARRY   Oh, come on, you've got to eat, you've got to eat. Keep up your strength. No, seriously, I would consider it a great honour. A great honour. Besides, there's nothing worse than eating alone, is there? Be nice if, just for once – the life I lead, I seem to spend my life eating alone.

PAULA   Well, when you're at home you don't . . .

HARRY   Ah, well. On those occasions, on those rare occasions . . . Matter of fact, to be frank, I'm not often there. I mean, I don't want to start boring you by talking about myself particularly but, well – let's just say I'm not very often at home. Enough said? Enough said. Cheers. (*Pause*) I mean, don't get me wrong. My wife and I, we're not separated, anything like that. It's just – well, to be perfectly honest she's a lot happier if I'm not at home too much. You might say, we no longer see eye to eye. If you follow my meaning. She's got very strong views on certain matters and, er – well there you are. I mean, I'm – as I was saying only a minute ago to Paula here – I'm by nature – easy going. However, it takes all sorts as they say. It so happens my wife is one of those people who considers that these sort of things cannot be forgiven or forgotten – ever. No matter. No matter how much you may talk to her or apologize to her about it. She's not a woman to take sorry for an answer. So there you are. I live there. On occasions. That's about all. But it's not life. I don't call that life. (*Pause*) Anyway, enough of my problems. (*Pause*) The point is this, if my wife were sitting here now with us all, she would have no claim over me whatsoever. Nor, let's be

perfectly honest, would I have on her. Washout.
Finish. Waiter, we'll have the same again, please.

The WAITER *approaches.*

BERNICE No, thank you very much.

PAULA No. Harry, Harry . . .

HARRY Waiter! Same again here.

BERNICE No, thank you very much. No more, Waiter.

HARRY Waiter, we want three more of the same.

PAULA No, honestly, Harry . . .

HARRY Three more, Waiter, we'll argue it out later.

WAITER Three more, sir.

The WAITER *departs.*

BERNICE I don't want any more.

HARRY Come on, that's only your first.

BERNICE That's all I want.

HARRY You've got to catch up with me and Paula, for
God's sake.

BERNICE I don't have to at all.

PAULA It's very kind of you.

HARRY Well, he's bringing them now, it's too late. You
needn't worry, it's on me. On me. I mean, I'm not
a big drinker either, you know. Don't get me
wrong. I'm not hooked on it. I can go for weeks
without a drink, you know, if I have to. Doesn't
bother me in the least. But, for God's sake, if I get
the chance of sitting here with two simply
stunning-looking creatures the like of which I
have never set eyes upon before, believe you me
– well, I think it calls for a drink. I don't drink at
home, you know. Never drink at home.

BERNICE You're never there.

HARRY I only drink socially. I only drink to be sociable.

No, never been my problem, drink. I've got other
problems but drink's not one of them. Thank God.
And I do very sincerely thank God. I won't go into
my other problems, I don't want to shock you.
(*He laughs.*) I mean, today, you won't believe that
today, I was drinking all lunchtime with a
colleague of mine, an old friend, a dear old friend
I hadn't seen for a very long time. We had a few
together over lunch, I won't deny that and I
happened to be in here again when they opened
the bar this evening. And I haven't even got a
thick head. Would you believe that? Incredible,
isn't it?

The WAITER *arrives with drinks.*

HARRY   Ah. Thank you very much, Waiter. Good man,
good man. Room two-four-nine.

WAITER   Two-four-nine, sir. Will that be all, sir?

HARRY   For the time being, thank you very much. (*As the*
WAITER *goes, he calls him back.*) Oh, Waiter. Here,
here – just a sec. (*Fumbling in his pocket and
producing a pound note*) Here's for yourself.

WAITER   Oh, that's very kind of you. Thank you very much,
sir.

HARRY   Have one yourself.

WAITER   Very kind indeed, sir.

The WAITER *goes.*

HARRY   Take care of them. They'll take care of you.
Cheers.

BERNICE   (*not touching her drink*): Cheers.

HARRY   No, I'll tell you both something now. I'll be
absolutely honest with you – now, I don't want you
to be shocked because the last thing I want to do
in this world to you two lovely girls is to shock you
but I have to say, you are both of you – now I'm
not in any way trying to get off with you, anything

like that, you are two of the most amazingly
startlingly sexy girls I have ever seen in my life.
Now that's no – no – sort of kidding at all. I want
you to believe that.

PAULA Thank you very much.

HARRY No, no, Paula my darling, I want to hear you say
you believe that. Will you say very clearly, I
believe that.

PAULA Yes, we do.

HARRY You do believe that, don't you?

PAULA Yes.

BERNICE *gives her a "come on" look.*

PAULA Harry, Bernice has got to meet her uncle at the
station.

HARRY Just a minute, let me finish . . .

PAULA She's got to meet her uncle at the station, you see,
Harry. The train's due in a few minutes.

HARRY No, well I'll get you down to the station, my
darling, don't you worry about that. I'll get you a
taxi.

PAULA No, Harry . . .

HARRY I'll buy you a taxi.

PAULA We have to go, Harry.

HARRY No. Listen, listen, Paula, Paula – Bernice. Listen.
This is not in any way an advance, it's not anything
like that, please believe that. I mean, I respect you
far too much, you see. I respect you as ladies.
Look, you see this . . . (*Holding up his room key*)
This is a key, right? The key to my room, two-four-
nine, which is a very, very nice room, believe me.
Now, I'm going to put this key down here in the
middle of the table, like that. Now, I'm going to
leave it there. I'm not going to try and embarrass
you, you see, but it's there. If you want to pick it
up, it's there there. Entirely up to you. Can't say

fairer than that.

BERNICE *rises.*

HARRY   Where are you going?

BERNICE   We have to go.

PAULA *tries to rise.* HARRY *pushes her down.*

HARRY   Paula, there's the key, you see.

PAULA   Yes, but you'll need it, Harry.

HARRY   No, I'll get another one. They have another one at the desk. This is for you.

BERNICE   Come on.

HARRY   If you want it, there it is.

PAULA   Thank you very much, Harry.

HARRY   Two-four-nine. If you want it, come and get it.

PAULA   Thank you, Harry. We have to meet her uncle, you see.

BERNICE   Paula, are you coming?

PAULA   Yes, I'm coming. (*She rises.*)

HARRY   (*catching* PAULA's *wrist*): Just a minute, just a minute. Waiter, Waiter.

PAULA   Wait.

The WAITER *arrives.*

HARRY   Waiter.

WAITER   Yes, sir?

HARRY   I wonder, Waiter, if you'd do me a favour. These two enchanting young ladies want to go to – where is it? – the railway station – to meet their uncle. Could you arrange them a taxi, do you think?

WAITER   The hall porter will get you a taxi, sir.

HARRY   Ah, well. Would you mind asking him very nicely.

WAITER   I'm sorry, sir, I'm not allowed to leave the bar.

HARRY   Oh, for crying out loud.

PAULA   It doesn't matter, Harry, don't bother.

BERNICE   Are you coming?

HARRY   What's the matter with this place?

PAULA   We'll walk, Harry, we can walk.

HARRY   You're not walking. I'm not having you walking, not on your own. I'm going to get you a taxi.

BERNICE   (*moving in*): We don't want a taxi, thank you.

HARRY   (*pushing her aside*): Wait there. (*Confidentially*) Paula.

PAULA   What?

HARRY   (*pushing the room key into her hand*): Here. You keep this. Understand. It's up to you. It's entirely up to you. I want you to know that. No strings. No strings at all.

PAULA   Thank you.

HARRY   (*blundering off*): I won't be a moment. Waiter, I'm relying on you to keep an eye on these magnificent girls.

WAITER   I'll do that, sir.

HARRY   Wait there.

     HARRY *goes through the saloon bar.*

BERNICE   Oh my God, I thought we'd never get rid of him.

PAULA   Awful when you get like that.

BERNICE   Thought you'd have learnt better by now. We'd better go quick.

PAULA   We can't. He's just out there.

BERNICE   (*to the* WAITER) Is there another way out, please?

WAITER   Yes, just through there, madam. There's a side door just through to your left.

BERNICE   Thank you. Right, come on, let's go.

PAULA   Good night.

WAITER   Good night to you, madam.

     The GIRLS *start to move off by the side door.*

WAITER Oh, madam, excuse me – you won't forget to leave the key, will you?

PAULA Oh. Nearly forgot. (*She hands him the key.*) Would you mind?

WAITER Not at all, madam. Good night.

PAULA *and* BERNICE *leave. The* WAITER *slips the key into his pocket and starts to clear the empties, as the Lights fade to a Blackout.*

BETWEEN MOUTHFULS

A hotel dining-room. Two tables are set apart, each with two chairs. Between them a service table. An IN and OUT door from the kitchens. The main entrance for Guests. The discreet clatter of knives and forks from other invisible diners. The WAITER *is finishing arranging his two tables. He wanders over and leans against the service table. At length,* DONALD PEARCE *enters, a middle-aged businessman.*

WAITER	(*approaching him*): Good evening, sir.
PEARCE	Good evening. I have a table for two reserved in the name of Pearce.
WAITER	Table for two, sir. Did you make a reservation, sir?
PEARCE	Yes, I've just said I did.
WAITER	Very good, sir. (*He consults the reservations book on the service table.*) What name was it, sir?
PEARCE	Pearce. I've just this minute said so.
WAITER	Pearce – with a P, I presume? – ah, yes, sir. (*Indicating the table nearer the door*) Would this one over here suit you, sir?
PEARCE	No, I don't think it would. I think I'd prefer this one over here.
WAITER	Oh, just as you like, sir.
	The WAITER *leads* PEARCE *over to the table and holds the chair for* PEARCE, *who sits, his back to the rest of the room.*
PEARCE	Thank you.
WAITER	Just yourself is it, sir?
PEARCE	No.

WAITER	Ah. Someone will be joining you, will they, sir?
PEARCE	Yes, indeed. That's really rather why I reserved a table for two.
WAITER	Right, sir.

The WAITER *goes to the service table to collect menus.* EMMA PEARCE *enters, same age as* PEARCE, *worried and tense. She catches sight of her husband and moves across to join him. The* WAITER *hurries across to help her with her chair.*

PEARCE	Oh, there you are.
WAITER	Good evening, madam.
MRS PEARCE	(*sitting*): Thank you. (*To* PEARCE) You might have waited for me.
PEARCE	I had absolutely no idea where you'd got to.
MRS PEARCE	You know perfectly well where I was.
WAITER	(*handing her a menu*): Thank you, madam.
MRS PEARCE	I told you.
WAITER	Thank you, sir.
PEARCE	Thank you.
MRS PEARCE	Oh lord. I suppose I've got to read through all this. (*She fumbles in her bag.*)
WAITER	Would you, madam, or yourself care for a drink before your meal, sir?
PEARCE	No, we wouldn't thank you.
MRS PEARCE	Oh no, I haven't brought them.
PEARCE	We may have some wine.
WAITER	Right, sir.
MRS PEARCE	That's that. I haven't brought them. (*She takes out a cigarette.*)
PEARCE	What?
MRS PEARCE	My reading glasses. I've left them at home.
PEARCE	I suppose that means I've got to read it to you.

The WAITER *lights* MRS PEARCE *'s cigarette.*

MRS PEARCE Unless you want me to guess.

PEARCE (*to the* WAITER): Would you bring us an ashtray, please.

WAITER Yes, sir.

PEARCE Why the hell can't you keep your glasses permanently in your handbag . . .

The WAITER *moves away. As he does so,* PEARCE *'s voice fades out. Throughout we hear only that dialogue that the* WAITER *himself hears when within earshot. Whether or not the* WAITER *registers the content of what he is hearing apart from remarks directly addressed to him, he never betrays.* PEARCE *continues speaking, but we can no longer hear him. The* WAITER *fetches the ashtray from the service table, dusts it, and returns to* PEARCE *'s table.*

MRS PEARCE (*fading out*): . . . this afternoon whilst I was reading and I forgot them, that's all.

PEARCE All right, all right, all right.

MRS PEARCE (*to the* WAITER): Thank you.

PEARCE And we'll have the wine list as well.

WAITER Wine list. Yes, sir.

PEARCE Now then, are you listening? Here we go. (*Reading*) Hors d'oeuvres from our trolley, grapefruit cocktail . . . (*He fades out.*)

The WAITER *returns to the service table for the wine list.*

POLLY *and* MARTIN *enter, a young couple.*

WAITER Good evening, sir. Good evening, madam. Just the two of you, is there?

MARTIN That's right.

WAITER Have you a reservation, sir?

MARTIN   No, we haven't.

WAITER   Just a moment, sir. (*He consults the book.*)

POLLY   I hope there's going to be room.

MARTIN   (*looking round the restaurant*): There'll be room. (*Catching sight of the* PEARCES) God, look who's here.

POLLY   Where?

MARTIN   Over there, look. Donald Pearce and his wife.

POLLY   Oh.

MARTIN   Better go and say hallo.

POLLY   No, don't do that.

MARTIN   What?

POLLY   Let's go somewhere else.

MARTIN   What?

POLLY   They'll feel they'll have to ask us to join them. Let's go somewhere else.

MARTIN   I'm not going somewhere else.

POLLY   They haven't seen us yet. Quick . . .

MARTIN   I'm not going somewhere else. What's the matter with you?

POLLY   I just don't feel like talking to them.

MARTIN   Why not?

POLLY   Not now.

WAITER   Sorry to keep you, sir. Would this table here be all right, sir?

MARTIN   (*as they follow him to the other table*): You can't expect me to cut my boss dead in a restaurant.

POLLY   We'll have to pretend we haven't seen them.

MARTIN   It's obvious we've seen them.

POLLY   Why? They haven't seen us. We could leave now.

    The WAITER *holds the chair for* POLLY.

MARTIN   I'm not leaving now. (*He sits. To the* WAITER) Thank you. (*To* POLLY) What's got into you?

POLLY   Nothing. (*She sits.*)

WAITER   Excuse me, sir.

MARTIN   I mean, I thought you always got on with them.

POLLY   They're all right.

WAITER   Excuse me, sir.

MARTIN   You used to be perfectly happy . . . (*To the* WAITER) No, thank you – perfectly happy to go round when they invited us.

POLLY   Not tonight. I don't feel like sitting down . . . (*She fades out.*)

The WAITER *returns to the service table and picks up the wine list. He moves to the* PEARCES' *table with it.*

PEARCE   (*fading up*): . . . Dover sole meuniere. Lobster thermidor. Lobster americaine brackets when in season. Scampi – all sorts of scampi – grilled halibut . . . (*He fades out.*)

The WAITER *has slipped the wine list down beside* PEARCE*'s elbow and departed. He returns to his service table, takes up two menus and crosses to* MARTIN*'s table.*

POLLY   . . . seen you for three weeks. I'd rather like it if we were just on our own.

MARTIN   I'm not the one who went away.

POLLY   All the same . . .

MARTIN   I mean, you're the one who went off on holiday. I didn't go off on holiday.

POLLY   You could have done. (*Taking her menu*) Thank you.

MARTIN   I couldn't, I told you. Old Pearce there – (*taking his menu)* – thank you – old Pearce there landed me with enough work to last me a year.

POLLY That wasn't my fault, Martin . . .

MARTIN I'm not saying it was. I was merely explaining why . . .

The WAITER *departs. He edged towards the* PEARCES' *table with his order pad.*

PEARCE . . . grilled pork chops, tournedos à la Crowne – whatever that may be – steak diane, grilled fillet steak brackets when available. Rump steak – Garni . . .

The WAITER *withdraws and leans against the service table, waiting. After a moment, he moves again to* MARTIN*'s table to see if any decision has been made there.*

MARTIN . . . book a holiday at a time when you know I'm going to be very busy.

POLLY Because if I waited for you not to be busy I'd never get a holiday at all.

MARTIN Come on, darling. This chap wants us to order.

WAITER No hurry, sir, no hurry.

POLLY I mean, it was either a case of my taking a holiday on my own or not having a . . .

The WAITER *wanders back to the* PEARCES.

PEARCE . . . roast Aylesbury ducking with orange sauce. Roast spring chicken with stuffing. Roast turkey with cranberry sauce . . .

The WAITER *withdraws.* MARTIN *signals for the* WAITER. *The* WAITER *moves to* MARTIN*'s table.*

POLLY . . . enjoy going on holiday on my own.

MARTIN Waiter, what's the Soup of the Day?

WAITER (*checking over* MARTIN *'s shoulder*) Er – minestrone, sir.

MARTIN (*unenthusiastically*): Oh.

MARTIN *and* POLLY *ponder their menus. The* WAITER *hovers.*

MARTIN How was the trip back?

POLLY Not bad. Had to be at the airport at seven this morning. We got to Heathrow at ten . . .

MARTIN Sorry I couldn't meet you.

POLLY I didn't expect you to.

MARTIN Our sales meeting went on till lunchtime.

PEARCE *signals and mimes Waiter.*

WAITER Yes, sir?

T*he* WAITER *moves across from* MARTIN *'s table to* PEARCE *'s.*

PEARCE Waiter, what is the Soup of the Day?

WAITER Minestrone, sir.

PEARCE Oh.
Pause.

WAITER Do you wish to order now, sir?

MRS PEARCE Do you do Eggs Benedict?

WAITER (*doubtfully; looking over* PEARCE *'s shoulder*): Eggs Benedict, madam . . .

PEARCE I should imagine that if they did Eggs Benedict, they'd have put Eggs Benedict on the menu.

WAITER I don't think we do, madam.

MRS PEARCE I was only asking.

PEARCE I mean, I read you the menu very distinctly. I didn't read out Eggs Benedict, did I?

MRS PEARCE I don't know.

PEARCE But I've just this minute finished reading it to you.

MRS PEARCE I don't know, I wasn't listening.

PEARCE (*taking a deep breath*): I think we need a few more minutes to decide, Waiter.

WAITER Very good, sir.

PEARCE I suppose you want me to read it to you all over again . . .

The WAITER *hovers back near* MARTIN *and* POLLY.

POLLY . . . marvellous the whole time. Baking hot. And it's a beautiful island.

MARTIN (*uninterestedly*): Yes. Sounds it. (*Seeing the* WAITER) Ah. Now then. So far we've got one pâté maison – one smoked trout. And you were . . .?

WAITER (*waiting*): Pâté maison – smoked trout.

POLLY Is the lobster fresh?

WAITER Oh yes, madam. I can recommend it.

POLLY Then I'll have Thermidor with a green salad.

MARTIN Poulet estragon for me.

WAITER Poulet estragon – thermidor. Would you care to see the wine list, sir?

MARTIN Might as well. My wife has just returned from the sunny Mediterranean. She's probably got the taste after three weeks.

WAITER Very nice, too, madam. Excuse me a moment, sir.

The WAITER *moves across again to the* PEARCES.

MRS PEARCE . . . the moment you come back you start.

PEARCE I'm not starting again. I was merely saying . . . (*Seeing the* WAITER) Yes?

WAITER I just wondered if you were ready with your order yet, sir.

PEARCE   No indeed, we are not ready with our order yet. We will let you know when we are.

WAITER   Very good, sir.

MRS PEARCE   Every single time you come back from somewhere, you're absolutely . . .

The WAITER *collects the wine list from the service table.*

MARTIN   . . . it was your idea.

POLLY   I didn't know they were going to be here, did I?

MARTIN   It was your idea we came out.

POLLY   Since the children were away, I thought it would be nice.

MARTIN   It was a lovely idea. Enjoy it.

POLLY   Yes, but I didn't know they were going to be here, did I . . .

PEARCE   (*calling*): Waiter!

The WAITER *returns to* PEARCE.

WAITER   Sir?

PEARCE   You will be pleased to hear that we have at last decided. Pencil at the ready. Here we go. One potted shrimps – one grapefruit cocktail and if it has a maraschino cherry on it, we don't want it. One Dover sole meuniere off the bone – one rump steak, just this side of medium rare . . .

WAITER   (*scribbling furiously*): Just a minute, sir – Dover sole off the bone – rump steak, medium rare . . . Have you decided on a wine, sir?

PEARCE   Oh – yes. (*He opens the list.*) White? Emma? White, do you want white?

MRS PEARCE   I don't mind either way. I only want half a glass.

PEARCE   Well, just say red or white?

MRS PEARCE I honestly don't mind. (*She looks out front.*)

PEARCE Red, then.

MRS PEARCE *turns sharply and glares at him.*

PEARCE Ah, now. What have you got in the Italian line?

WAITER I think they're at the back here, sir. The wine waiter's not on at the moment, otherwise . . .

PEARCE Ah yes, here we are, Italian. We had a very very reasonable one at the hotel where we stayed.

MRS PEARCE I thought you went there to work.

PEARCE I did go there to work. I had to stop occasionally. Now then.

MRS PEARCE My husband's been overworking in Italy, poor thing . . .

PEARCE No, you don't seem to have it.

MRS PEARCE I don't know how you managed to work in all that blazing sunshine.

PEARCE A bottle of this one here, the – er – one-oh-four.

WAITER Oh right, sir. The – er – one-oh-four. Yes, sir.

MRS PEARCE How on earth did you manage to cope for three whole weeks . . .?

The WAITER *goes out through to the kitchens and after a second, returns. He takes up some cutlery, places it on a tray and crosses to* MARTIN*'s table.*

MARTIN . . . last six months are beginning to move. Somebody up there seems to have our interests at heart, anyway.

WAITER Smoked trout, madam?

MARTIN No, that's me – and not before time, as far as I'm concerned. Old Pearce was back this afternoon, full of the joys of spring, anyway. I don't know what he got up to in Rome but he seems to have had a good time of it.

The WAITER *exchanges some of* POLLY *'s and* MARTIN *'s cutlery, replacing it with a fish knife and fork.*

POLLY I thought he went on business.

MARTIN I can't believe it took him three weeks to get a contract signed. I know the Italians are difficult . . . mind you, I think if I was married to Emma Pearce, I'd chase off to Rome.

POLLY Don't stare.

MARTIN It's all right, he's got his back to us. And she's as blind as a bat.˙No, he probably had some little Italian señora lined up there. He always likes to mix his business with a bit of . . .

The WAITER *goes to* PEARCE *'s table.*

WAITER Potted shrimps, sir?

PEARCE Thank you.

WAITER And a steak for madam?

PEARCE No, that's for me as well.

A pause while the WAITER *exchanges cutlery, replacing* MRS PEARCE *'s with a fish knife and fork, and* PEARCE *'s with an outer fish knife and fork and a steak knife.*

MRS PEARCE Well, I'm sorry, I don't believe you.

PEARCE That's up to you. (*Pause*) That what I was doing.

MRS PEARCE I'm sorry, I think you're a liar.

The WAITER *crosses to* MARTIN *and* POLLY.

MARTIN . . . and the problem was to re-allocate staff work schedules so that everyone was guaranteed at least one day off in three whilst guaranteeing normal production.

POLLY Yes.

WAITER Excuse me, sir.

MARTIN Which was one hell of a problem. Yes?

WAITER Have you chosen a wine, sir?

MARTIN (*picking up the wine list*): Oh yes – you see, as soon as you say, lost men off the assembly section, you had to insure you had sufficient manpower to tide you over the entire three-day period without any noticeable shrinkage in labour effectiveness.

POLLY Martin, he's waiting to know what wine.

MARTIN Oh yes. Do you do a carafe?

WAITER Yes, sir.

MARTIN A carafe of white. Not too sweet.

WAITER Carafe of the white, sir.

MARTIN Anyway, we managed it. We put in the report and Donald Pearce is over the moon. I mean, he only had time to glance at it this afternoon but . . .

The WAITER *goes into the kitchens. The* PEARCES *sit in silence.* MARTIN *chatters to* POLLY. *The* WAITER *returns with the* PEARCES' *first courses, grapefruit cocktail, potted shrimps, plate of toast. He crosses to* PEARCE'S *table.*

WAITER Grapefruit cocktail, madam?

MRS PEARCE Thank you.

WAITER Potted shrimps, sir.

PEARCE Thank you.

MRS PEARCE I'm sorry, I think you're lying.

WAITER Beg your pardon, madam? Oh, I'm sorry, madam, I beg your pardon. Toast is there, sir.

The WAITER *returns to the kitchens. The* PEARCES *eat,* MARTIN *continues to talk. The* WAITER *returns with* MARTIN'S *and* POLLY'S *first courses. He goes to their table.*

MARTIN . . . so in the end I did the only thing possible. I took on entire responsibility for the whole A, D and J project. Took on both jobs. Did the lot myself.

POLLY   Yes, I know, you told me this before, Martin.

The WAITER *serves her with pâté.*

POLLY   Thank you.

MARTIN   When did I tell you? (*He leans forward over the table.*)

The WAITER *tries unsuccessfully to slip the plate under* MARTIN*'s hands.*

POLLY   I've only been away three weeks, you know.

MARTIN   What time are we picking up the kids?

POLLY   I told Gran we'd be there in time for lunch.

MARTIN   Ah well, end of peace and quiet. (*He leans back.*)

The WAITER *quickly slides* MARTIN*'s plate into place.*

MARTIN   Thank you.

POLLY   Did you miss them?

MARTIN   I honestly haven't had a moment to miss anyone, love. Not even you.

POLLY   I missed them dreadfully.

WAITER   (*fiddling at the table*): Toast is just there, madam.

POLLY   Thank you.

MARTIN   Oh, did I tell you, Graham Shotter finally got that job in Glasgow.

POLLY   Oh, did he . . .

The WAITER *goes to the kitchen, returning with both the carafe and* PEARCE*'s wine. He puts the carafe down on the service table, wipes the bottle, shakes it upside down, then takes it to* PEARCE*'s table and holds it out for his inspection.*

WAITER   Sir. The one-oh-four, sir.

PEARCE Oh yes. (*He reads the label very carefully, muttering all the words to himself, including the name of the shippers.*) Righto, yes.

WAITER Thank you, sir.

The WAITER *produces a cork-screw from his pocket and starts to open the bottle by their table.*

PEARCE Did you get someone in to look at that radiator in the bedroom?

MRS PEARCE They said they'd come on Tuesday.

PEARCE Oh.

MRS PEARCE He said it sounded as if it needed a new part.

PEARCE That's out.

The WAITER *pulls out the cork with a "pop".*

PEARCE I'm not paying for a new part. I'm not wasting my money on that.

MRS PEARCE Just on holidays. (*She lights another cigarette.*)

The WAITER *pours a little wine into* PEARCE *'s glass.*

PEARCE Are you deliberately trying to annoy me this evening?

WAITER Would you care to try it, sir?

PEARCE Oh . . . (*He sips his glass.*) Bit on the chill side. It'll do. Go ahead.

WAITER Thank you, sir.

The WAITER *starts to pour wine for* MRS PEARCE.

MRS PEARCE That's enough, thank you.

WAITER Thank you, madam.

PEARCE Are you eating that or just leaving it?

MRS PEARCE Leaving it.

The WAITER *pours* PEARCE *the rest of his glass and puts the bottle on the table.*

WAITER   I'll leave it here, sir. Finished, madam?

MRS PEARCE   Yes, thank you.

PEARCE   Was it all right for you, madam?

MRS PEARCE   Beautiful. I'm just not very hungry.

WAITER   (*removing her plate*): Thank you, madam.

PEARCE   I don't see any point in ordering food if you're not going to eat it . . .

The WAITER returns to the service table, picks up the carafe of wine and crosses to MARTIN and POLLY's table.

POLLY   I just think it's a terrific cheek, that's all.

MARTIN   No, honestly, love, it isn't really I – thank you –

The WAITER starts to pour wine for POLLY. She picks up her glass while he is still pouring.

MARTIN   The quality of the wife is frightfully important. If you've got a top executive virtually responsible for what? – two or three hundred men sometimes – it's vitally important that he's married to the right woman.

POLLY   Why?

MARTIN   Well, that he has a stable relationship. That she's suddenly not going to walk out on him.

The WAITER picks up MARTIN's glass and fills it, so that MARTIN cannot touch it until he has finished pouring.

POLLY   She's going to take no part in his work, is she?

MARTIN   Well, hardly, no.

POLLY   Then I think the firm ought to mind its own bloody business, I'm sorry . . .

The WAITER moves away, PEARCE finishes. The WAITER moves in to take his plate.

MRS PEARCE   I said, who is she?

PEARCE   Who is who?

MRS PEARCE   Who is she?

PEARCE *opens his mouth to reply then becomes aware of the* WAITER. *The* WAITER *takes away his plate and puts it on the service table. He sees* POLLY *and* MARTIN *have finished and goes to remove their plates.*

POLLY   . . . what I'm saying is, that as far as I'm concerned, you could be manufacturing – marmalade. You spend all day in the office, you work at home most of the night, you never talk to the children and I don't even know half the time what it is that you're doing.

MARTIN   Look, darling, you wouldn't understand if I told you . . .

The WAITER *takes the empty plates to the kitchen.* PEARCE *and* MRS PEARCE *are having a short, terse conversation.* MARTIN *talks agitatedly.* POLLY *looks slightly desperate. The* WAITER *returns with the* PEARCES' *second course: rump steak for him, Dover sole for her, and vegetables. He goes to their table.*

PEARCE   I don't think this is quite the occasion for this sort of conversation, do you?

MRS PEARCE   I can't think of any better time.

PEARCE   In a public restaurant.

MRS PEARCE   Why not?

WAITER   Dover sole, madam.

MRS PEARCE   Thank you.

PEARCE   I don't see any point in causing a scene . . .

MRS PEARCE   I am not causing a scene. I asked you a perfectly normal question. Who is this woman?

WAITER   Rump steak, sir.

PEARCE	What does it matter?
MRS PEARCE	Because I want to know.
PEARCE	Who said there was anyone, anyway?
MRS PEARCE	Oh, come along, darling, I am not a fool. I am not a bloody fool.
PEARCE	Would you mind lowering your voice.
MRS PEARCE	I will not lower my voice.
WAITER	Runner beans, madam?
MRS PEARCE	No, thank you. I want nothing else.
WAITER	No potatoes either, madam?
MRS PEARCE	(*shrilly*): Nothing else.
WAITER	Very good, madam. (*He moves round to* PEARCE.)
PEARCE	(*to* MRS PEARCE, *fiercely*) Could you kindly try and control yourself.
WAITER	Runner beans for you, sir?
PEARCE	(*snarling at him*): Yes please.
MRS PEARCE	Well, I'll tell you one thing, darling, if I ever get my hands on the little whore, I'll wring her neck.
PEARCE	Do you mind, do you mind.
WAITER	Carrots, sir?
PEARCE	Yes.
MRS PEARCE	You can tell the little bitch that from me.
WAITER	Potatoes, sir?
PEARCE	No. No potatoes. Nothing else.
WAITER	Very good, sir.
PEARCE	Nothing else, at all.
WAITER	Right, sir.

The WAITER *moves away and returns to the
kitchens. Both tables are in a fair state of
animation. The* WAITER *returns with* POLLY'*s*

and MARTIN *'s main courses: lobster, chicken, salad dressing, salad, vegetables. He moves to their table.*

POLLY   . . . that's what it boils down to. I'm not in the slightest bit interested in your work and you don't give a damn what I'm up to. There we are. We haven't one thing in common.

MARTIN   Oh, come on, I don't know.

The WAITER *serves* POLLY*'s lobster.*

POLLY   Thank you.

MARTIN   I'm interested in what you're up to.

POLLY   Really?

MARTIN   Of course . . .

POLLY   Nonsense.

MARTIN   It's not nonsense at all.

WAITER   (*serving*): Poulet estragon, sir.

POLLY   These last three weeks I was away, were you the slightest bit interested in where I was?

MARTIN   I know where you were.

POLLY   Do you?

MARTIN   You were in – wherever it is – Majorca.

POLLY   I was not in Majorca, darling, as it happens. I was in Rome.

WAITER   Vegetables, sir?

MARTIN   Er – just carrots. Rome? What were you doing in Rome?

POLLY   I was with Donald Pearce.

MARTIN   Donald Pearce – that's fine, thank you – what were you doing with Donald Pearce?

POLLY   I spent three weeks with Donald Pearce in a hotel in Rome.

MARTIN   My God. (*He puts his head in his hands on the*

table.)

WAITER	Potatoes, sir?
MARTIN	Oh my God.
WAITER	(*bending right down to speak to* MARTIN): Excuse me, sir.
POLLY	(*to the* WAITER): No, he doesn't.
WAITER	Oh, right, madam.
POLLY	(*to* MARTIN): I'm sorry.
WAITER	Sorry, madam?
POLLY	Nothing.
WAITER	Oh, sorry, madam. Green salad.
MARTIN	Oh my God.
POLLY	Thank you.
WAITER	French dressing, madam?
POLLY	Yes, just a little . . .
MARTIN	How could you do it?
POLLY	I don't know. I'm sorry. I felt – I don't know . . .
MARTIN	You realize what you've done?
POLLY	It's not important, darling, it's all over. That's why I told you.
MARTIN	It may be all over for you. What happens when she finds out?
POLLY	Who?
MARTIN	Emma Pearce. You realize what's going to happen to me.
POLLY	What?
MARTIN	I'll be out on my ear. As soon as Emma Pearce gets wind of – oh, damn it. If you were going to choose someone why the hell did it have to be Donald Pearce? That's it, don't you see? That's the end of everything. The end of my prospects of promotion. I shall probably be forced to resign.
POLLY	Is that what's worrying you?

MARTIN   Of course it's what's worrying me.

WAITER   Is that sufficient for you, madam?

POLLY   Oh, for crying out loud, I can't believe it – I just can't believe it. (*She stands, pushing back her chair.*)

MARTIN   Where are you going?

POLLY   Don't you care anything for me? Nothing at all?

MARTIN   Where are you going?

POLLY   I'm going to be physically sick.

POLLY *storms out.*

WAITER   Was everything all right for madam, sir?

MARTIN   Yes, it was fine, fine. Thank you very much.

WAITER   Thank you, sir.

The WAITER *moves away and crosses to the* PEARCES' *table with the intention of topping up the wine glasses, trying not to be noticed.*

PEARCE   For the last time, will you pull yourself together.

MRS PEARCE   I'll kill her when I see her, I'll kill her.

PEARCE   Don't be so stupid. (*Seeing the* WAITER, *sharply*) What do you want?

WAITER   I was – just going to pour some more wine, sir.

PEARCE   We can do that ourselves. Go away.

WAITER   Just as you like, sir. (*He starts to go.*)

MRS PEARCE   Waiter.

WAITER   Madam?

MRS PEARCE   (*indicating her plate*): You can take this away.

WAITER   Have you finished, madam?

MRS PEARCE   Yes, it was quite delicious, thank you very much. (*She gets up.*) Excuse me.

WAITER   Was everything all right, madam?

MRS PEARCE   Perfectly. It's just I'm afraid I'm unable to enjoy a meal with a man who turns out to be a deceitful, lecherous liar.

MRS PEARCE *flips* PEARCE*'s plate into his lap.* PEARCE *leaps up.* MRS PEARCE *goes out of the restaurant hurriedly, blowing her nose. She passes by* MARTIN *without seeing him.* MARTIN, *sitting stunned, does not see her.*

PEARCE (*dabbing at his trousers with his napkin*): Oh, for the love of mike.

WAITER I'll get a cloth, sir. Just a minute.

PEARCE Look at this, look at this. Where's the Gents? I'll have to mop up.

MARTIN *rises.*

WAITER Just through here, sir. I'll show you.

The WAITER *leads* PEARCE *to the door past* MARTIN*'s table.* MARTIN *has risen.*

PEARCE Damn fool thing to do. What a damn . . . (*He bumps into* MARTIN.) Excuse me, I – good God, hallo, Chalmers.

MARTIN Oh, hallo, Mr Pearce.

PEARCE I didn't know you were here. Excuse me, I've just had a bit of a mishap.

MARTIN Oh, good heavens, yes.

PEARCE Having a night out, are you?

MARTIN Yes, yes, that's right.

PEARCE So are we. Well, have to unwind once in a while, don't you?

MARTIN Rather, rather . . .

PEARCE Are you still eating, or are you . . .?

MARTIN No, I was just . . .

PEARCE Well, I'll tell you what. I've just got to have a quick mop up in the Gents. Won't be a second. Then –

fancy a quick brandy in the bar?

MARTIN Oh, that would be very nice indeed, Mr Pearce.

PEARCE Just a quick one . . . (*To the* WAITER, *who is still mopping at his trousers.*) All right, that'll do, Waiter, thank you. Could you bring the bill through to the bar, please.

WAITER Yes, of course, sir.

PEARCE Oh, and you can put them all on to one if you like.

MARTIN Oh, that's most generous of you, sir.

PEARCE Not at all, not at all. I think after all that stalwart work you've done on that report I probably owe you a meal, don't I?

MARTIN Oh, I don't know about that . . .

The WAITER *moves out of earshot.* PEARCE *claps* MARTIN *on the back. The* WAITER *starts to clear the* PEARCES' *table.* PEARCE *and* MARTIN *leave the restaurant,* PEARCE *with his hand on* MARTIN'*s shoulder, both laughing and talking animatedly. The* WAITER *looks out front, as – the Curtain falls.*

GOSFORTH'S FÊTE

A tea tent. One long trestle table, the odd bench or collapsible chair. In one corner near one of the entrances, a jerry-rigged rather large valve-type amplifier with wires leading from it to outside. Another entrance at the other end of the table. MILLY, *a fresh-faced pink woman, staggers in with a box of teacups. She is wearing an overall-coat. She dumps the cups on the table. She attempts to assess the number in the box without removing them. She is involved with this when* EMMA PEARCE *comes in through the other entrance. She is now smartly turned out in a feather hat, light raincoat, white gloves with smart matching bag and shoes.*

MRS PEARCE	Excuse me.
MILLY	I'm sorry, I'm afraid we're not serving teas for another two hours. Can I help you at all?
MRS PEARCE	Well, I'm Emma Pearce.
MILLY	Em – oh golly. Councillor Mrs Pearce.
MRS PEARCE	That's right.
MILLY	Oh, Golly. Um. Well. Has nobody met you?
MRS PEARCE	No. I saw one or two people. They seemed rather busy.
MILLY	Oh, yes . . .
MRS PEARCE	I parked just in the lane there. Is that alright?
MILLY	Fine. I should think. I'm afraid we're all a bit behindhand.
MRS PEARCE	Yes. Well, Mr – er Gosfirth . . .
MILLY	Gosforth, yes . . .
MRS PEARCE	He did say in his letter two-fifteen.
MILLY	He should be about – somewhere. He was. I'm Milly Carter.

They shake hands.

MRS PEARCE How do you do.

MILLY It's very nice of you to come.

MRS PEARCE Quite all right.

MILLY Is your husband any better?

MRS PEARCE Better?

MILLY Yes. Hasn't he been ill?

MRS PEARCE No.

MILLY Oh. I thought that's why he couldn't come. Sorry.

MRS PEARCE No. It's just he had some business to see to. He couldn't get away. At the last minute.

MILLY Oh, I see.

MRS PEARCE So you'll have to make do with me, I'm afraid.

MILLY Yes . . . Oh, no. Not at all. We all tremendously appreciate your being here. Really. Super. Really.

MRS PEARCE Thank you.

MILLY And it's for a jolly good cause.

MRS PEARCE Yes, indeed.

MILLY I mean, it's just what this place needs – a new village hall. Did you pass the old one on your way here? You probably did.

MRS PEARCE Was that the building on the . . .?

MILLY Yes. Just along the lane there. I mean, frankly it's an eyesore. It was put up during the war. All corrugated iron. If you're holding a meeting and it rains, you might as well save you breath.

MRS PEARCE Oh dear. The weather looks a little threatening today.

MILLY Yes. I do hope it doesn't rain. I mean, we can house quite a lot of our activities in the marquee over there – or even in this tea tent if the worst came to the worst, but there's things like Mr Stokes's Wolf Cubs' P.T. display –

you couldn't fit that in here for instance.

MRS PEARCE   Were those Wolf Cubs, all those little boys out there in gym vests?

MILLY   Yes. Were they behaving themselves?

MRS PEARCE   They were throwing stones at a caravan. I told them to stop it.

MILLY   Oh lord, good for you. They won't take a blind bit of notice. They're all little horrors. Every one of them. But thanks for trying. No, you see it's vital we get a good attendance. Absolutely vital. Mr Gosforth has worked tirelessly. I'm o/c teas. Tea lady for the day. I usually teach at the school.

MRS PEARCE   Oh, how interesting.

MILLY   Quite a challenge, I can tell you. Most of the children round here are as thick as two planks. We don't seem to have any budding village genius . . .

The sound of GOSFORTH*'s voice is heard off, through a loud-hailer, shouting "Keep off there, you boys".*

MILLY   Oh, here's Mr Gosforth.

MRS PEARCE   Ah.

GOSFORTH *enters. He is beery-faced, shirtsleeved, perspiring, at present a born leader of men. In one hand, he carries a battery-operated loud-hailer, in the other, a plastic carrier-bag filled with clinking bottles. He looks as if he is in the thick of battle. As soon as he has entered, he turns and glares out through the tent entrance.*

GOSFORTH   (*bellowing through his loud-hailer*): Will all you Wolf Cubs come down off that scaffolding at once. This is your last warning. (*Lowering the loud-hailer and turning into the tent*) Bloody little vandals, swarming all over it like . . . (*Seeing* MRS PEARCE) Ah . . .

MILLY Mr Gosforth, this is Councillor Pearce.

GOSFORTH Oh good lord, hallo. (*He puts the loud-hailer on the table and shakes hands.*)

MRS PEARCE How do you do.

GOSFORTH Gordon Gosforth. So nice of you to come. Sorry I wasn't here to meet you. Been having a bit of guy-rope crisis.

MRS PEARCE Oh dear.

GOSFORTH We rented both these damn tents, you see. Didn't really open them up until today. Didn't have the space. When we do, we find half the guy ropes are missing off the main marquee – this one's safe enough – had to do an emergency job. Not a window left in the district with any sash cord. (*He laughs.*) Now, the curriculum goes as follows. Two-thirty p.m. we plan to kick-off. I'll give you a short introduction – needn't be too long – as soon as you've finished – up strikes the band – got them coming over from Hadforth – they should be here – why aren't they? – then if you can mingle about a bit if you don't mind a spot of mingling – have a go at bowling for the pig – just seen Fred Crake's trailer so the pig's arrived safely, thank God – roll a few pennies and all that sort of thing – then, at three-thirty – if you can stay till then – I hope you can – Second Little Pendon Wolf Cubs' P.T. Display, organized by Stewart Stokes – that should go on for about half-an-hour – four o'clock tea, courtesy Milly Carter and assorted ladies – four-thirty, soon as they've swallowed their biscuits – novelty races, fathers' race, mothers' race, three-legged grandfathers' race, all that sort of rubbish – five-thirty to six – final round-off with an organized sing-song with the Hadforth Band – has the Reverend managed to get the song-sheets run off? – ten pounds to a quid he hasn't –

six o'clock all pack up, dismantle tents – seven-thirty all cleared away because old Swales wants the field back for his cows first thing in the morning. Hope you can stay for a bit of the fun.

MRS PEARCE   Yes.

GOSFORTH   Sure you'll want to. Milly, where is that blasted man Fairchild?

MILLY   He said he'd be back. He had to go on a call.

GOSFORTH   He had better be back. Not a solitary thing is working. (*To* MRS PEARCE) Penalty of having a local quack who is also the electrical expert. (*He indicates the amplifier.*) Rigged up the entire sound system – got all the wires down – microphones – amplifier there, you see – loud-speakers, the lot. Only trouble is, not a bloody thing's working. Now he's taken off on some emergency.

MRS PEARCE   Oh dear.

GOSFORTH   Oh dear, indeed. If he doesn't fix it when you make your speech nobody'll hear a word you're saying . . .

There is a rumble of thunder.

GOSFORTH   That sounds ominous. Milly, my darling . . .

MILLY   Yes, Gordon?

GOSFORTH   (*handing her the carrier-bag*): These are some prizes for the races. Half a dozen bottles of sherry. Could you hide them behind the counter where the Cubs can't get at them. (*To* MRS PEARCE) Advantages of running a pub. Ready-made prizes always to hand. (*He catches sight of something going on outside the tent behind her.*) Excuse me a minute. (*Snatching up the loud-hailer and shouting through it*) Reverend, over here. Reverend, would you mind . . . (*Lowering the loud-hailer, to* MRS PEARCE) Useful gadget this. Saves the voice. Would you like a look round before we start, Councillor Mrs Pearce? We may be a few minutes. I think you'll find it impressive. What there is of it so far, anyway.

MRS PEARCE Lovely.

The VICAR *enters, laughing. He laughs a lot, especially when he is nervous.*

VICAR (*laughing*): Hallo there. Bad news, I'm afraid, Gosforth.

GOSFORTH What's happened?

VICAR I've been finally let down on the song-sheets, I'm afraid.

GOSFORTH (*clasping his head*): Oh – (*inaudibly*) – help us. Pardon the language.

VICAR No, the man who owned the duplicator has gone out of business.

GOSFORTH Oh well. Delete community singing. Insert community humming.

VICAR (*laughing*): Community humming, I like that . . . (*Seeing* MRS PEARCE) Oh, I beg your . . .

GOSFORTH I'm so sorry. Councillor Mrs Pearce, this is John Braithwaite, our vicar.

MRS PEARCE How do you do.

They shake hands.

VICAR How do you do. Very kind of you – to turn out. And how is your husband? Better, I hope.

MRS PEARCE He's not ill.

VICAR Oh dear, seriously?

MRS PEARCE No, he's not ill.

VICAR Oh, I beg your pardon. I thought you said he got ill. He's not ill. That's better.

MRS PEARCE Yes.

VICAR There's a big difference between not ill and got ill, isn't there? No, we don't want to get those two confused.

GOSFORTH John, I wonder if you'd like to show Councillor Mrs Pearce the lie of the land. Take her for a turn round the tombola.

VICAR Of course. Delighted.

GOSFORTH If you'll excuse me, Councillor – I think I'll have to pitch in to this public address system – see what I can do with it myself.

MRS PEARCE Yes, of course.

GOSFORTH Twelve loudspeakers strung all the way round the field and not a squeak out of any of them.

VICAR Would you care to follow me, Councillor?

MRS PEARCE Yes, of course. See you later.

MRS PEARCE *exits.*

GOSFORTH Yes indeed. And Vicar, would you tell those confounded Wolf Cubs to come down off that scaffolding. It was only built for loud-speakers, you see.

VICAR I will, I will.

GOSFORTH They're not designed to take that sort of weight, you see.

VICAR Quite. Point taken.

The VICAR *exits.*

GOSFORTH In fact, as far as I can make out, they're not designed to take any sort of weight. Now then, how's my little Milly, all right?

MILLY I think we're all right. Old Mr Durban is bringing the tea urn over in a minute.

GOSFORTH Splendid. Now then . . .

Thunder.

GOSFORTH   Oh, grief. Hark at that. Now then, where do I start
           with this lot. (*He looks at the amplifier on the floor.*)
           The amplifier seems to be working okay. (*He turns
           on the light.*) Well, anyway, the light's on . . .

MILLY   Gordon . . .

GOSFORTH   (*involved*): Just a second, lovey . . . I'd better start
           at the business end and work round. Loose
           connection somewhere. That's all it can be. (*He
           starts to examine the mike plugs and lead, testing
           them from time to time.*) Hallo, hallo, one, two,
           three, four, five.

MILLY   Gordon, have you a minute, please?

GOSFORTH   Hallo, hallo. Where the hell's that damn fiancé of
           yours got to?

MILLY   I don't know.

GOSFORTH   Well, I wish he'd stick around. He could have
           helped me sort this out. He's never around when
           you need him. Those damn Wolf Cubs of his are
           running amok.

MILLY   Gordon, have you got a minute? Please . . .

GOSFORTH   (*sitting on a chair, still fiddling with the mike*):
           Darling girl, does it look as if I've got a minute?

MILLY   It's frightfully urgent, Gordon.

GOSFORTH   All right, old girl, go ahead. I'll just keep fiddling.

MILLY   Well . . . (*She pauses.*)

GOSFORTH   Uh-huh . . .

MILLY   It's really rather awful. It does seem terribly as if
           perhaps I might be pregnant.

GOSFORTH   Oh yes.

MILLY   Yes.

           GOSFORTH *drops the mike, as he realizes what she has*

*said. The jolt causes the mike to become live. We
hear, distantly, their voices echoing away on a
series of loudspeakers. They alone, in their concern,
remain unaware of this.*

GOSFORTH	Did you say pregnant?
MILLY	I'm frightfully sorry.
GOSFORTH	Me?
MILLY	There's no-one else it could have been, Gordon.
GOSFORTH	Oh my God. (*He rises, with the mike.*)
MILLY	I'm really awfully sorry. What are we going to do?
GOSFORTH	Well . . .
MILLY	What am I going to say to Stewart?
GOSFORTH	Oh . . .
MILLY	He'll be dreadfully upset.
GOSFORTH	Yes, I can see he might, yes.
MILLY	He might refuse to marry me.
GOSFORTH	Yes, I can see he might, yes.
MILLY	(*her lip trembling*): I don't know what to do.
GOSFORTH	Now, easy, easy, Milly. (*He puts his arm round her.*) Now you're absolutely sure.
MILLY	Yes.
GOSFORTH	Yes. Well. This needs thinking about.
MILLY	What's Stewart going to say when he finds out? What's it going to do to him? Everyone knows we're engaged. How's he going to face his Cubs?
GOSFORTH	Well, he's a good bloke. He's a Scout, isn't he, after all. He's pretty decent. Now listen, Milly, we must just get through today first. Then we'll talk about it. You see?
MILLY	Yes.
GOSFORTH	Don't worry.
MILLY	No.
GOSFORTH	You're not to worry, we'll sort it out. But first

things first. You get your tea organized and I'll see
if I can get this wretched thing to – one, two,
three – ah, success, it's working – don't know
what it was I did but I – ah . . .

They look at each other, appalled.

MILLY   How long's it been on for?

GOSFORTH   Very good point.

STEWART STOKES *enters in full Scout kit. Normally a
pink young man – he is now red with fury.*

MILLY   Stewart . . . !

STEWART   You bastard, Gosforth . . .

GOSFORTH   Hallo, old boy.

STEWART   You complete and utter bastard, Gosforth.

GOSFORTH   Now keep calm, Stokes.

STEWART   I'm going to kill you, Gosforth.

GOSFORTH   Stokes, keep calm.

STEWART   With my bare hands.

GOSFORTH   I warn you, Stokes, this thing is live.

STEWART   Well, switch it off, you coward, switch it off.

GOSFORTH   I don't know how to switch if off.

STEWART   Haven't you done enough? How do you think it
feels to hear the news that my fiancée is pregnant
by another man? Isn't that bad enough? But
when you publicly announce it over four acres of
field . . . in front of all my Cubs . . .

GOSFORTH   I say, Stewart, I'm sorry.

STEWART   There are Brownies out there as well, you know.

GOSFORTH   This is still on, Stewart, this is still on.

STEWART *throws down his Scout's pole, seizes the
mike and tries to wrest it from* GOSFORTH*'s hand.*

STEWART   And turn it off! Turn it off!

GOSFORTH   Steady, steady, steady. This thing is still on. Milly, turn it off. Turn it off!

MILLY   Wait, wait, stop it. (*She switches the amplifier off.*) It's off now. It's off.

GOSFORTH   Thank God.

MILLY   Stewart, we'll have to talk about this later.

STEWART   I do not want to talk about this later. I do not want to talk about it at all.

MILLY   Stewart, please. It's no help to anyone getting in a state.

GOSFORTH   She's quite right, Stewart old man, she's quite right.

STEWART   (*collapsing in a chair, almost in tears*): Four acres – four acres . . .

GOSFORTH   Steady, Stewart, old boy, steady. We'll sort it out, I promise. We'll sit down later and sort it out. Milly, crack open one of those bottles of mine, would you? Give him a glass of sherry.

STEWART   I don't drink. You know I never drink.

GOSFORTH   Well, you're in need of one now, Milly . . .

MILLY   Yes, just a minute.

MILLY *opens a bottle and pours some into a cup. The* VICAR *sticks his head into the tent.*

VICAR   Excuse me.

GOSFORTH   Yes, Vicar?

VICAR   Were you aware that your ill-tidings were being broadcast abroad?

GOSFORTH   Yes. Thank you, John, we were aware.

VICAR   I see. Oh dear. I'm dreadfully sorry . . .

GOSFORTH   Yes. Thank you, John, thank you.

The VICAR *goes.*

GOSFORTH Oh well, sorry, Milly. There goes your reputation as spinster of this parish.

STEWART That's not funny, Gosforth.

GOSFORTH Sorry, old boy, sorry.

MILLY (*bringing over the cup and bottle of sherry*): Here . . .

GOSFORTH Here we are. Drink up, old boy, drink up.

STEWART *drinks reluctantly.*

MILLY Perhaps he ought to lie down in the first-aid tent.

STEWART I don't want to lie down.

GOSFORTH The first-aid tent isn't up yet. Someone's swiped one of their poles.

STEWART I've got things I have to do.

MILLY What?

STEWART I haven't finished the platform.

It starts to rain.

GOSFORTH You haven't? Oh lord.

MILLY What platform?

GOSFORTH The platform upon which Councillor Mrs Pearce is supposed to make her speech twenty minutes ago. We need that finished. Can't start at all otherwise.

MILLY Well, can't someone else . . .?

STEWART It's all right. I'll do it, I'll do it.

GOSFORTH (*at the tent flap*): Oh no. Here comes the wretched rain.

MILLY Oh no.

Thunder.

MILLY Oh, just look at it. Nobody'll come and the ones that are here will go home.

GOSFORTH   Dear oh dear. Like a monsoon. Hang on, I'll try
          raising their morale. Try and keep them here
          somehow. (*He snatches up the loud-hailer and
          stands in the doorway.*) This is only a short
          shower. Please feel free to shelter in the main
          marquee. I repeat this is only a short shower. (*He
          lowers the loud-hailer.*) I don't think that
          convinced anybody.

MILLY   (*suddenly*): Oh heavens.

GOSFORTH   What is it:

MILLY   I left the biscuits out the back . . .

          MILLY *hurries out, after picking up a newspaper to
          protect her hair.* STEWART *sits drinking.*

GOSFORTH   I wouldn't drink too much of that, Stewart old
          boy, if you're not used to it.

STEWART   Go to hell, Gosforth, you fascist.

GOSFORTH   Your platform's getting a bit damp out there. Want
          a hand to drag it in?

STEWART   Go to hell, Gosforth, you swine.

GOSFORTH   All right, I'll drag it in.

          GOSFORTH *goes out, as* MILLY *comes in with a
          cardboard box of biscuits.*

MILLY   Phew! Just saved them in time. Could you give
          me a hand, Stewart? Stewart . . .

STEWART   Hah!

MILLY   Oh, well. Don't then . . .

          MILLY *goes out.* GOSFORTH *comes in through the
          other doorway, dragging* STEWART*'s platform. A
          small, square rostrum with a rail like a wayside
          pulpit.*

GOSFORTH   Pity to let this get ruined. You put a lot of effort into
          this. Never seen such a shower out there. The lucky-

dip tub's like a water-butt already. What was left to
do on this, Stokes? Stokes? Oh, come on, stop sitting
there feeling sorry for yourself, Stokes . . .

MILLY *staggers in with a second box of biscuits,
holding the wet newspaper on her head.*

MILLY Could one of you give Mr Durban a hand with the
tea urn? He seems to have got bogged down in the
mud by the gate. he's stuck.

GOSFORTH All right, all right, I'll go. No use expecting our Boy
Scout to do anything.

GOSFORTH *goes out through the other door.*

MILLY Oh, Stewart, honestly, just sitting there leaving poor
old Mr Durban to cope. He's over seventy, you
know – and those Wolf Cubs of yours are throwing
mud at each other. I wish you'd try and control
them. They should be taking shelter. Oh well, don't
blame me if they all go down with pneumonia.

STEWART What made you do it, Milly?

MILLY What?

GOSFORTH With a man like – Gosforth? That fascist . . .

MILLY Oh, don't drag politics into it, Stewart, for goodness'
sake.

STEWART What made you do it, Milly?

MILLY (*brightly*): Oh, I don't know. Can't remember
now.

STEWART What do you mean, you can't remember?

MILLY (*taking the newspaper from her head*): Well, I
suppose I can, yes. It was while you were off at the
Scout Jamboree.

STEWART Oh God . . .

MILLY I went across to the pub to get some brandy – for
Mother – she thought she had a cold coming. She

wanted some in her hot milk.

STEWART Go on.

MILLY Well – Gordon was there, behind the bar as usual.
It was a quiet evening for some reason. No-one in
the saloon at all. He offered to buy me a drink.

STEWART He got you drunk. (*He takes another swig.*)

MILLY No, he didn't. Not very, anyway. Not as drunk as
you'll get if you keep going at that the way you are.

STEWART Typical. Got you drunk and then took advantage
of you.

MILLY Do you want to hear what happened or not?

STEWART No. Yes – I don't know.

MILLY Anyway. It sort of got later – and – Mother didn't
get her brandy. Gordon closed up the bar and we
sat on in there talking. He told me all about his
ex-wife and I talked about you.

STEWART You talked to him about me? Us?

MILLY Yes.

STEWART How dare you talk to that man about us.

MILLY Oh, for heaven's sake, Stewart, if you're going to be
righteously indignant, do take off that stupid hat.

STEWART This is not a stupid hat.

MILLY It is on you.

STEWART This is my badge of office.

MILLY And those absurd baggy shorts.

STEWART You always said you liked me in my uniform . . .

MILLY Well, I don't any more.

STEWART I don't know what's got into you, Milly.

MILLY I don't either. I've grown up, I think. I'm thirty-
four, pregnant by a man I don't much care for and
I've grown up. And not before bloody time . . .

MILLY *goes out.* STEWART *stands unsteadily, adjusts his*

uniform and pours himself another drink. The VICAR *enters holding a notice-board over his head which reads: "Grand Fête Today 2.30 p.m." In his other hand, a microphone stand.*

VICAR My goodness, my goodness. Ah, Stewart.

STEWART Hallo, Vicar.

VICAR You – er – heard the broadcast – I take it?

STEWART Yes. I did.

VICAR I'm sorry. Not the most tactful way to hear that sort of news.

STEWART No.

VICAR It must have come as a great shock to you.

STEWART To everyone. Everyone heard it, you know.

VICAR Ah, yes. But then everyone knew it, you see. Except you, that is.

STEWART They did?

VICAR Oh, yes.

STEWART How?

VICAR Well, it's a very small village, isn't it? And the spectacle of Miss Carter being let out at the side door of the "Fox and Hounds" at six a.m. on a Sunday morning is not all that common an occurrence.

STEWART I see.

VICAR If you hadn't been at your Jamboree, I . . . (*Holding up the mike stand*) I brought this in with me. I don't know if it's vital to anything.

STEWART Oh yes, it's the microphone stand, I think.

VICAR Ah. Well. Your Wolf Cubs appear to be rolling in the mud.

STEWART Let them. Who cares.

VICAR Well, no, they're enjoying themselves. I don't know what their mothers are going to say. All those clean white P.T. vests.

GOSFORTH *staggers in with the tea urn, followed by* MILLY.

MILLY Can you manage?

The VICAR *goes to help, but burns his hand on it.*

GOSFORTH Yes – weighs a ton . . . (*Dumping it down on the end of the table*) Right. That's it. There we are.

MILLY It's a good job you rescued him. Old Mr Durban had sunk in up to his knees.

VICAR Oh dear.

GOSFORTH Well now. Change of plan is called for, I think – Stewart, will you lay off that stuff. I think in view of the weather an early tea is called for. Can you manage that, Milly?

MILLY Yes, I think so, I've seen Mrs Winchurch around somewhere. She can help me. My other ladies weren't due till three-thirty.

GOSFORTH And what the hell's happened to the Hadforth Band? They should have been here half an hour ago. Right. Revised schedule of event one. Opening speech by Councillor Mrs Pearce . . .

MILLY In the rain?

GOSFORTH She needn't get wet. We can put that platform in the tent entrance there – she can stand just inside the doorway. Anyway, even if they can't see her they can hear her. As soon as she's through – tea. Then we just pray that by the time we've finished that, this lot will has passed over. We'll have to scrub round the gym display – I don't think the instructor's quite up to it anyway.

STEWART Go to blazes, Gosforth. (*He drinks again, from* *the bottle.*)

GOSFORTH And to you, old boy. Now then, let's – where the devil is she?

MILLY Who?

GOSFORTH Councillor Mrs Pearce? Where is she? What did you do with her, Vicar?

VICAR Oh. Yes. I think I rather lost sight of her during the – broadcast. I thought she was – that's odd. Oh dear.

GOSFORTH (*snatching up his loud-hailer and marching to the door*): Councillor Mrs Pearce. Would Councillor Mrs Pearce kindly report to the tea tent. (*Lowering the loud-hailer*) She can't have got far.

VICAR I'll see if I can find her.

VICAR *runs out with his notice-board over his head. A big clap of thunder is heard.* GOSFORTH *starts fixing the mike into its stand which he arranges in front of the platform in the doorway.* MILLY *starts to put out a few cups and saucers.*

MILLY I wonder how many there's going to be of them?

GOSFORTH How many cups have you got there?

MILLY About three hundred and fifty.

GOSFORTH Well, I should start with about six. (*Examining the amplifier.*) My God, the rain's getting on to this thing. It'll short out completely if we're not careful. (*He moves it to the side of the table.* STEWART *obstructs him.*) Look Stewart, would you mind . . . Milly, will you get your boy-friend out of the road, please.

STEWART I'm not her boy-friend.

MILLY He's not my boy-friend.

The VICAR *returns.*

VICAR No sight nor sound of her. I hope she's all right.

GOSFORTH	Where the hell has she got to? She can't have vanished into thin . . .

MRS PEARCE enters through the other door. Her feather hat is limp, her shoes and stockings coated in mud. She is exhausted and soaked. MILLY stifles a scream.

GOSFORTH	Councillor Mrs Pearce!
VICAR	Good heavens.
MRS PEARCE	Oh. At last . . .
VICAR	Do sit down, Mrs Pearce, please.
MILLY	What happened to you?
MRS PEARCE	(*breathless*): I went – I saw your church – I thought I had time to take a quick look . . .
VICAR	Yes, yes. You're very welcome to.
MRS PEARCE	It started raining – I found I'd lost my sense of direction. One of your Wolf Cubs finally directed me . . .
VICAR	Good boy, good boy . . .
MRS PEARCE	The wrong way. I finished up in a ploughed field.
GOSFORTH	Typical. Pack of little vandals . . . Mrs Pearce, if you're feeling up to it, I really feel we ought to start the ceremony – for what it's worth. Then we can get on with our tea.
MRS PEARCE	All right.
GOSFORTH	Feeling fit?
MRS PEARCE	Yes, yes.
GOSFORTH	Right, then. Let's get weaving. With or without the Hadforth Band, blast them. (*Switching on the amplifier*) Just pray this thing's still working.
STEWART	You swine, Gosforth.
GOSFORTH	(*ignoring STEWART*): So far so good. (*He climbs on the platform. He taps the mike experimentally.*) One –

two – three – four – success. Good afternoon to you, ladies and gentlemen – boys and girls. (*Breaking off as he sights something*) Will you Wolf Cubs not persecute that pig, please. Now keep well clear of the pig – thank you. (*Resuming*) May I first of all thank you all for braving the elements this afternoon and coming along here to support this very worthwhile cause. That cause is, as we all know, the building of the new village hall. Something that eventually can be enjoyed by each and everyone of us in this community. I won't keep you longer than I have to – I'm well aware this is hardly the weather for standing about and listening to speeches. We will, in view of the circumstances, be altering our programme of events slightly. We plan to take tea in the tea tent, that is the tent from which I am speaking to you now, immediately after we have heard from our distinguished Guest of Honour. She herself needs very little introduction I am sure. Both she and her husband have served as councillors for this ward for many years and during that time have, I feel – and here I'm speaking over and above any purely party political feeling – have, I feel, done tremendous work both for us and for that whole community to which we all belong. Without further ado, may I call upon Councillor Mrs Pearce formally to open this Grand Fête. Councillor Mrs Pearce.

GOSFORTH *steps down to make room for* MRS PEARCE. *Meanwhile, under this previous speech*:

VICAR (*to* MILLY, *in a whisper*): Do you think it would be very wicked of me to sneak a cup of tea now?

MILLY (*whispering*): Not at all. Help yourself.

VICAR (*whispering*): Thank you. I will.

MILLY *returns her attention to the speech. The* VICAR *goes over and takes a cup. Anxious not to get in anyone's way, he swivels the urn round so that the tap is directly over the amplifier. He turns on the tap and starts to fill his cup.* STEWART, *now lying on the ground, starts to sing softly.*

MILLY   (*to* STEWART): Ssh.

VICAR, *having poured his tea, finds he is unable to turn off the tap of the tea urn.*

VICAR   Oh dear.

MILLY   Ssh.

VICAR   Help!

MILLY   What?

VICAR   I can't turn off the tap.

MILLY   Oh. Wait . . .

MILLY *dashes over, hands him another empty cup to catch the flow and takes the full one from him. They continue this chain of filling cups, in between time trying vainly to stem the flow of tea from the urn without success. This continues until* GOSFORTH *has finished his speech. As soon as he has done so,* MRS PEARCE *steps on to the rostrum.*

MRS PEARCE   Ladies and gentlemen. I seem to have brought the wrong weather with me, I'm afraid. But this is an occurrence which I don't think for once you can blame on either me or the Conservative Party. It reminds me very much of a saying my husband is very fond of quoting. The rain in Spain may indeed fall mainly on the plain – but what's left of it seems to fall mainly in Kent. Joking apart, and I don't want to turn this into a political occasion in any way – but since we have been in control of your Council – I think everyone here will agree with me – the Conservatives have made startling progress – (*gripping the microphone*) – progress not only for the rich among you but also for the not so well off – not only for the rich man in his castle – but also for the poor man at his gate – if I may, I'd like to take a brief look at our recent record on Council Housing. Over three hundred new houses in less than two years. Compared, I may remind you, with the previous Labour best of only a hundred and fifty Council houses. In other words, a hundred per cent increase. Startling indeed . . .

Under the above:

GOSFORTH (*in an urgent whisper*): What the blazes are you doing?

MILLY It's stuck.

GOSFORTH What's stuck.

MILLY The tap's stuck.

VICAR Could we possibly turn it upside down?

GOSFORTH Why the hell don't you leave things alone?

STEWART *has found the loud-hailer and begins to croon through it, softly at first, a selection of camp-fire songs.*

STEWART Ging gang gooly gooly gooly gooly watcha . . .

GOSFORTH Shut up, Stokes! Milly, get that off him.

MILLY (*who is preoccupied running to and from with cups*): How can I?

GOSFORTH (*wrestling with the tap*): Damn and blast this thing.

STEWART Here we sit like birds in the wilderness . . .

MILLY Shut up, Stewart.

STEWART (*at* MRS PEARCE): Ring-wing fascist propaganda.

GOSFORTH	Stokes! Someone get him out of here.
STEWART	Long live the Revolution!
GOSFORTH	(*moving away from the urn*): Just a minute. Keep things going, keep things going . . .

GOSFORTH *goes to* STEWART, *takes the loud-hailer off him and drags him roughly to his feet.*

GOSFORTH	Come on, you, come on.
STEWART	Kindly do not molest me, you adulterer.
GOSFORTH	Come on. Out in the fresh air. (*He drags* STEWART *to the other entrance.*)
STEWART	Baden-Powell for President.
GOSFORTH	Come on.
STEWART	Home Rule for Wolf Cubs.

GOSFORTH *drags* STEWART *out.* MILLY *and the* VICAR *continue to drain off the urn into a growing number of cups.*

MILLY	We're never going to drink all this tea.
VICAR	Quickly, please, quickly.
MILLY	I'm being as quick as I can.

GOSFORTH *returns, wiping his hands.*

GOSFORTH	That's fixed him. Right. Next job. Now stand clear, Vicar, stand clear.
VICAR	I don't think I should. I might . . .
GOSFORTH	(*pushing him back*): Please stand clear.

GOSFORTH *wrestles with the tap afresh. With the* VICAR's *cup no longer there to catch it, the tea pours into the amplifier below. There is a loud buzzing and howling noise from the loud- speaker system.* MRS PEARCE, *who is holding the mike and still in full flow, suddenly begin*

both physically and vocally to oscillate violently.
GOSFORTH *manages to turn off the urn.*

GOSFORTH   Done it! (*Aware of the din*) What the hell's
           happening?

MILLY   Look . . . (*She points to* MRS PEARCE.)

VICAR   Good gracious. (*He runs to* MRS PEARCE.) Mrs
           Pearce . . .

The VICAR *and* GOSFORTH *lever* MRS PEARCE *away from
the mike. The* VICAR *grabs the stand and gets a
shock.*

GOSFORTH   Steady, Vicar, steady . . .

GOSFORTH hits the VICAR*'s hand from the stand, and
turns in time to catch* MRS PEARCE, *who collapses.*

GOSFORTH   Give us a hand, Milly.

MILLY   (*going to do so*): Right.

GOSFORTH   Are you all right, Councillor Mrs Pearce?

MRS PEARCE (*weakly quavering*): The Conservative Party have
           always striven . . .

GOSFORTH   Vicar, can you and Milly lift her over to the first-
           aid people?

VICAR   Very well, very well.

GOSFORTH   I'll hold the fort here.

MRS PEARCE We have always believed in a fair deal for
           everyone . . .

MILLY   All right, Mrs Pearce.

GOSFORTH   Where the hell's that bloody Hadforth Band? It's
           never here when you want it.

MILLY and the VICAR *assist* MRS PEARCE *towards the
other exit.*

VICAR   We'll take her to the first-aid tent.

MILLY   It's not up.

GOSFORTH   Then tell them to get it up. This is an emergency.

MILLY, *the* VICAR *and* MRS PEARCE *go out.*

GOSFORTH   (*surveying the scene for a second*): Oh dear God
. . . (*He snatches up the loud-hailer and jumps on
to the platform.*) Ladies and gentlemen. Sorry
about this. Just goes to show these little technical
hitches can happen to the best of us. There's
going to be another slight alteration in our
schedule. In fifteen minutes, at three-fifteen, we'll
be having the home-made cake judging
competition in the main marquee, and after . . .

There is a loud crash.

GOSFORTH   Oh my God. Now I warned you Wolf Cubs, that
scaffolding was unsafe. Please stand back,
everyone. Let the first-aid people through. Please
stand well back . . .

There is the sound of a brass band approaching.

GOSFORTH   Oh dear God, what a time to turn up. (*Through the
loudhailer again*) Hadforth Band! Hadforth Band!
There are Wolf Cubs on the ground requiring
minor medical attention – would you please be
very careful where you match. I repeat, please be
very careful where you are marching . . .

*He leans on the platform rail which promptly drops
away. As he falls through the tent entrance, the
Lights fade to a Blackout.*

A TALK IN THE PARK

A park. Four park benches, separated but not too distant from each other. On one sits BERYL, *a belligerent young girl at present engrossed in reading a long letter. On another sits* CHARLES *who looks what he is, a businessman dressed for the weekend. He is slowly thumbing his way through a thick report. On another sits* DOREEN, *middle-aged, untidily dressed, feeding the birds from a bag of breadcrumbs. On the remaining bench sits* ERNEST, *a younger man. He sits gazing into space. The birds sing. After a moment,* ARTHUR *enters. He is a bird-like man in a long mackintosh, obviously on the look-out for company. Eventually, he approaches* BERYL'*s bench.*

ARTHUR	Is this seat occupied, by any chance?
BERYL	(*shortly*): No. (*She continues to read.*)
ARTHUR	Great, great. (*He sits.*)
	A pause. ARTHUR *takes deep breaths and gives a few furtive glances in* BERYL'*s direction.*
ARTHUR	Student, I see?
BERYL	What?
ARTHUR	Student, I bet. You look like a student. Always tell a student.
BERYL	No.
ARTHUR	Ah. You look like one. You're young enough to be a student. Quite young enough. That's the life, isn't it? Being a student. Not a care in the world. Sitting in the park on a day like this. In the sunshine. Rare enough we see the sun, eh? Eh? Rare.
BERYL	Yes. (*She refuses to be drawn into conversation.*)
ARTHUR	Mind you, I shouldn't be here. By rights, I should

bc at home. That's where I should be. Inside my
front door. I've got plenty of things I should be
doing. The kitchen shelves to name but three.
Only you sit at home on a day like today. Sunday.
Nothing to do. On your own – you think to
yourself, this is no good, this won't get things
done – and there you are talking to yourself. You
know what they say about people who talk to
themselves? Eh? Eh? Yes. So I thought it's outdoors
for you, else they'll come and take you away.
Mind you, I'm never at a loss. I'm a very fulfilled
person. I have, for example, one of the biggest
collections of cigarette cards of anyone alive or
dead that I know of. And you don't get that by
sitting on your behind all day. But I'll let you into
a secret. Do you know what it is that's the most
valuable thing there is you can hope to collect?
People. I'm a collector of people. I look at them, I
observe them, I hear them talk, I listen to their
manner of speaking and I think, hallo, here's
another one. Different. Different again. Because I'll
let you into a secret. They are like fingerprints.
They are never quite the same. And I've met a
number in my lifetime. Quite a number. Some
good, some bad, all different. But the best of
them, and I'm saying this to you quite frankly and
openly, the best of them are women. They are
superior people. They are better people. They are
cleaner people. They are kinder-hearted people. If
I had a choice, I'd be a woman. Now that makes
you laugh, I expect, but it's the truth. When I
choose to have a conversation, I can tell you it's
with a woman every time. Because a woman is
one of nature's listeners. Most men I wouldn't
give the time of day to. Now I expect that shocks
you but it's the truth. Trouble is, I don't get to
meet as many women as I'd like to. My particular
line of work does not bring me into contact

with them as much as I would wish. Which is a pity.

BERYL *gets up.*

BERYL   Excuse me. (*She moves off.*)

ARTHUR   Are you going?

BERYL *moves to* CHARLES'*s bench.*

BERYL   (*to* CHARLES): Excuse me, is this seat taken?

CHARLES   (*barely glancing up*): No. (*He moves along his bench.*)

BERYL   (*sitting*): Thanks. Sorry, only the man over there won't stop talking. I wanted to read this in peace. I couldn't concentrate. He just kept going on and on about his collections or something. I normally don't mind too much, only if you get a letter like this, you need all your concentration. You can't have people talking in your ear – especially when you're trying to decipher writing like this. He must have been stoned out of his mind when he wrote it. It wouldn't be unusual. Look at it. He wants me to come back. Some hopes. To him. He's sorry, he didn't mean to do what he did, he won't do it again I promise, etc., etc. I seem to have heard that before. It's not the first time, I can tell you. And there's no excuse for it, is there? Violence. I mean, what am I supposed to do? Keep going back to that? Every time he loses his temper he . . . I mean, there's no excuse. A fracture, you know. it was nearly a compound fracture. That's what they told me. (*Indicating her head*) Right here. You can practically see it to this day. Two X-rays. I said to him when I got home, I said, "You bastard, you know what they did to my head?" He just stands there. The way he does. "Sorry," he says, "I'm ever so sorry." I told him. I said, "You're a bastard, that's what you are..

A right, uncontrolled, violent, bad-tempered
bastard." You know what he said? He says, "You
call me a bastard again and I'll smash your stupid
face in." That's what he says. I mean, you can't
have a rational, civilized discussion with a man
like that, can you? He's a right bastard. My friend
Jenny, she says, "You're a looney, leave him for
God's sake. You're a looney." Who needs that?
You tell me one person who needs that? Only
where do you go? I mean, there's all my things –
my personal things. All my – everything. He's even
got my bloody Post Office book. I'll finish up back
there, you wait and see. I must be out of my tiny
mind. Eh? Sometimes I just want to jump down a
deep hole and forget it. Only I know that
bastard'll be waiting at the bottom. Waiting to
thump the life out of me. Eh?

CHARLES   Yes. Excuse me. (*He gets up.*)

BERYL   I'm sorry, I didn't mean to embarrass you.

CHARLES   No, no.

BERYL   I just had to . . .

CHARLES   Quite all right. Quite all right.

CHARLES *moves over to* DOREEN.

CHARLES   (*to* DOREEN): Nobody here, is there?

DOREEN   What?

CHARLES   Nobody here?

DOREEN   Where? (*She looks round.*)

CHARLES   Sitting here.

DOREEN   No. No.

CHARLES   Sorry. Do you mind if I do? (*He sits.*) I won't
disturb you. Girl over there's got boy-friend
trouble. Comes and pours it all out on me –
as if I'm interested. I mean, we've all been
through it at one time or another. Why she
should think I should be interested. I mean,

we've all got troubles no doubt. But we all don't
sit on a bench and bore some poor innocent
stranger to death. I mean, that in my book spells S
for selfishness. And have you noticed that it's
invariably the young? They think we haven't been
through it. Can't imagine that perhaps we were
young, too. Don't know where they think we all
came from. I mean, five years ago I had a house
in the country, a charming wife, two good
children, couldn't imagine a happier family. My
wife dies suddenly, my children can't stand the
place a moment longer and emigrate to Canada so
I sell the house and there I am in a flat I can
hardly swing a cat in. But I don't go round boring
other people with it. That's life. I've had twenty –
no, more like twenty-five, good years. Who am I
to complain if I get a few bad ones thrown in as
well. Make no mistake. I know I'm in for some
bad ones. Things are going to get worse before
they get better. Bound to. And you know an
interesting thing about trouble? I always think it's a
bit like woodworm. Once you've got a dose, if
you're not careful, it starts to spread. Starts in your
family and, before you know it, it's into your
business. Which explains why I'm sitting here
reading a report that's been put together so badly
that I've got to read it through on my one day off
and condense it into another report before I can
even be certain whether I'm bankrupt. I mean, I
don't know if you're interested but just look at this
page here, this is a typical page. Can you make
head or tail . . .

DOREEN *gets up and moves away.*

CHARLES   (*muttering*): Oh, I beg your pardon.

DOREEN *moves to* ERNEST'*s bench.*

DOREEN Excuse me.

ERNEST Eh?

DOREEN Excuse me. May I sit here for a moment? (*She sits.*) The man over there has been – you know – I didn't want to make a scene but he – you know. I mean, I suppose I should call the police – but they'd never catch him. I mean, most of the police are men as well, aren't they? Between you and me, I have heard that most of the police women are as well. Men dressed up, you know. Special Duties, so called. So my ex-husband informed me. I mean, it's terrible, you can't sit in a park these days without some men – you know – I mean, I'm on a fixed income – I don't want all that. That comes from my husband. My ex-husband. He runs a pub. In the country. But I had to leave him. We got to the stage when it was either that or – you know. I love dogs, you see, and he would never – he refused, point blank. And the day came when I knew I must have a dog. It became – you know – like an obsession. So I left. I usually have my dog here with me only he's at the vet's. He's being – you know – poor little thing. He'd have seen that man off. He's a loyal little dog. He understands every word I say to him. Every word. I said to him this morning, Ginger-boy, I said – you're coming down to the vet's with me this morning to be – you know, and his little ears pricked up and his tail wagged. He knew, you see. I think dogs are more intelligent than people. They're much better company and the wonderful thing is that once you've got a little dog, you meet other people with dogs. And what I always say is that people who have dogs they're the nicest sort of people. They're the ones I know I'd get on with.

ERNEST *gets up.*

DOREEN   Have you got a dog, by any chance?

ERNEST *ignores her and creeps behind the trees to*
ARTHUR.

ERNEST   (*sitting down next to* ARTHUR): Excuse me. Just
taking refuge. Nut case over there. Bloody woman
prattling on about her dog. Ought to be locked
up. Thinks every man's after her. I mean, look.
Look at it. After her? She'd have to pay 'em. You
know the sort though, don't you? If you let her
talk to you long enough, she'll talk herself into
thinking you've assaulted her. Before you know it,
she's screaming blue murder, you'll be carried off
by the fuzz and that's your lot. Two years if you're
lucky. I mean, I came out here to get away from
the wife. Don't want another one just like her, do
I? I mean. That's why I'm in the park. Get away
from the noise. You got kids? Don't have kids.
Take my tip, don't get married. Looks all right, but
believe me – nothing's your own. You've paid for
it all but nothing's your own. Yap, yap, yap. Want,
want, want. Never satisfied. I mean, no word of a
lie, I look at her some mornings and I think,
blimey, I must have won last prize in a raffle.
Mind you, I dare say she's thinking the same. In
fact, I know she is. Certainly keeps me at a
distance. Hallo, dear, put your money on the table
and she's off out. Don't see her for dust. Sunday
mornings, it's a race to see who can get out first.
Loser keeps the baby. Well, this morning I made it
first. Here I am in the quiet. Got away from the
noise. You know something interesting? Most of
our lives are noise, aren't they? Artificial man-made
noise. But you sit out here and you can listen – and

– well, there's a bit of traffic but apart from that –
peace. Like my mother used to say. Shut your eyes
in the country and you can hear God breathing.
(*He shuts his eyes.*)

ARTHUR   (*leaning across to* BERYL): Hey – hey – psst! I've got
a right one here. Thinks he's listening to God
breathing . . . (*He laughs.*)

BERYL   (*leaning across to* CHARLES.): He's talking again. To
me. What do you do? (*She smiles.*)

CHARLES   (*leaning across to* DOREEN): There she goes again.
What did I tell you? Chapter Two of the boy-friend
saga.

DOREEN   (*leaning across to* ERNEST): He's talking to me. If he
does it any more, I'll call the police . . .

ERNEST   (*to* ARTHUR): Oh, blimey. Why doesn't she go
home? Hark at her. Can you hear her? Rabbitting
on . . .

           The following, final section is played as a Round.
           DOREEN *finishes first, then* CHARLES *cuts out, followed
           by* BERYL, ARTHUR, *and then* ERNEST.

ARTHUR   (*to* BERYL): Hey – hey.

           BERYL *continues to ignore him.*

ARTHUR   Oh, suit yourself.

BERYL   (*to* CHARLES): Psst – psst.

           CHARLES *ignores her.*

BERYL   Oh, be like that.

CHARLES   (*to* DOREEN): I say, I say.

           DOREEN *ignores him.*

CHARLES   Oh, all right, don't then . . .

DOREEN   (*to* ERNEST): Excuse me, excuse me, excuse me.

ERNEST *ignores her.*

DOREEN Oh, really.

ERNEST (*nudging* ARTHUR): Oy – oy.

ARTHUR *ignores him.*

ERNEST Oh, all right, then. Don't. Don't then. Might as well talk to yourself.

They all sit sulkily. The Lights fade to a Blackout, and – the Curtain falls.

ACTIVITIES AND EXPLORATIONS

1 Keeping Track

The questions in this section are designed to help your reading and understanding of the plays in areas of plot, structure, character and interaction. They may be used as you read the plays or afterwards, for discussion or for writing. Some are developed and expanded in the **Explorations**.

Mother Figure

1 What is Lucy trying to do at the start of the play?
2 Why does she ignore both the telephone and the doorbell?
3 How does Lucy react to Rosemary during their conversation?
4 How does Rosemary react to Lucy during their conversation?
5 What do we learn of the state of Lucy and Harry's marriage?
6 What sort of drink does Rosemary think she is being offered? How does she react to what she is actually offered?
7 How is Terry meant to look to the audience?
8 "I don't think she's well." What gives Rosemary this idea about Lucy?
9 What do we learn about Terry's attitudes about men's and women's roles?
10 What do we learn about the state of Rosemary and Terry's marriage?
11 How does Lucy start to treat Rosemary and Terry? Why?
12 How does Terry react? Why?
13 How does Rosemary react? Why?

14 Why does Rosemary burst into tears?

15 How does Lucy comfort her?

16 How does Terry react to what he sees on his return?

17 How does Lucy force her will upon Terry?

18 Why does Terry start to behave childishly?

19 What happens onstage while Harry is on the telephone?

Drinking Companion

1 What is the link with the previous play?

2 How much has Harry been drinking? And how much has Paula been drinking?

3 What is Harry's attitude to Paula?

4 What is Paula's attitude to Harry?

5 Why does Harry tell the Waiter to charge the drinks to his room? And why does he tip him with a "handful of silver"?

6 What stages does Harry go through in trying to pick up Paula?

7 How does Paula react? Why?

8 How does Paula greet Bernice?

9 What type of character is Bernice?

10 Paula says Harry is "one of those". What does Bernice understand by this?

11 How does Bernice's arrival change Harry's behaviour?

12 What is Bernice's attitude to Harry?

13 How much does Harry drink?

15 How much do Paula and Bernice drink?

16 Why does Harry tip the Waiter with a pound?

17 How does Harry behave as Paula and Bernice prepare to leave?

18 Why does Harry fail in what he intends?

Between Mouthfuls

1 What is the link with the previous play?
2 What sound effects are needed at the start of the play?
3 What is the Waiter's attitude to his guests?
4 What is Pearce's mood?
5 What do we learn of the relationship between Pearce and Mrs Pearce?
6 How much dialogue does the audience hear?
7 How do Martin and Polly react when they see the Pearces are in the restaurant?
8 Where has Polly been for the last three weeks?
9 How interested is Martin in what Polly has to say?
10 Where has Pearce been recently?
11 Why does Pearce choose red wine?
12 How interested is Polly in what Martin has to say?
13 What effect does the Waiter's behaviour have on the two couples?
14 How do we learn the truth about Pearce and Polly?
15 How does Martin react to Polly's statement about her holiday in Rome? More importantly for Martin, why?
16 Why is Polly forced to leave the restaurant?
17 How do Pearce and Martin react when they meet?
18 'The Waiter looks out front'. What attitude, if any, should the Waiter convey to the audience?

Gosforth's Fête

1 What is the link with the previous play?
2 How well are the preparations proceeding for the fête?
3 How does Milly treat Mrs Pearce?
4 How well is Gosforth coping with his preparations?
5 What type of person is the Vicar?

6 What is the effect of dropping the microphone?

7 What is Gosforth's attitude to Milly a) before and b) after she has told him that she is pregnant?

8 What would happen onstage after Stewart's entrance?

9 Why does Ayckbourn insist on a growing storm outside?

10 How does the sherry affect Stewart?

11 How did the liaison between Milly and Gosforth occur?

12 What happens in the tea tent while Gosforth is delivering his speech?

13 What happens in the tea tent while Mrs Pearce is delivering hers?

14 How is Mrs Pearce electrocuted?

15 How does the fête end?

16 How far do the events in the fête match the events in the characters' lives?

A Talk in the Park

1 How does Beryl respond to Arthur? Why?

2 How does Charles respond to Beryl? Why?

3 How does Doreen respond to Charles? Why?

4 How does Ernest respond to Doreen? Why?

5 How does Arthur respond to Ernest? Why?

6 What is the significance of the final line of the play?

2 Explorations

The questions in this section are more detailed and rely on your having read the play through. Some of the questions develop ideas from the **Keeping Track** section: because they are more detailed they offer the opportunity to develop them into written, oral or practical coursework assignments. Some will require a close knowledge of the play; others will require an imaginative response.

A Characters

Mother Figure

1 How does the initial description of each of the characters in the stage directions introduce each character?

2 How much neighbourly contact is there usually between the Oateses and the Comptons? Explain your answer. What does this tell us about the characters?

3 'Whatever he has to say to me, he can say it to my face or not at all.' Give a detailed account, with reference to the text, of the state of Harry and Lucy's marriage. (Refer if you wish, to 'Drinking Companion'.)

4 What impression of Terry is the audience/reader intended to form?

5 What is Rosemary's attitude to her marriage to Terry?

6 How does Lucy succeed in dominating first Rosemary, then Terry?

7 How believable is the change in Rosemary's and Terry's behaviour? How does Ayckbourn set about achieving this change?

8 Script the conversation that might take place when Rosemary and Terry return home. Would their experience with Lucy have changed anything?

Drinking Companion

1   'You might say, we no longer see eye to eye.' What is Harry's attitude to his marriage with Lucy?

2   What impression of Harry is the audience/reader intended to form?

3   How does Harry set about attempting to seduce Paula and later Bernice? Why does he fail?

4   What type of characters are Paula and Bernice? Is it important that Bernice is 'a few years older' than Paula?

5   How do you think Paula and Bernice intend to spend their evening once rid of Harry? Script an incident that shows their characters in a situation that suits them better later that evening.

6   Back in his room, Harry believes that he has got through to his wife. What would he say to her? How would he say it?

Between Mouthfuls

1   How do Pearce and Mrs Pearce feel about each other? How do they show what they feel about each other?

2   What are Martin's principal concerns in life?

3   What is Polly's attitude to Martin?

4   How do the moods change at the Pearces' table during the course of the meal? Trace their development.

5   How do the moods change at the Chalmers's table during the course of the meal? Trace their development.

6   Script the conversation that would occur in the bar between Pearce and Martin.

7   If Polly and Mrs Pearce were to end up alone together in the Ladies' Powder Room, would they recognise each other? What might happen if they did?

8   How important is the Waiter's contribution to the events at each table?

Gosforth's Fête

1 What does the way that Milly treats Mrs Pearce and Gosforth tell us about her character?

2 How does Gosforth treat Milly before she tells him that she is pregnant? And afterwards? Why?

3 Explain Stewart's reaction to Milly's pregnancy.

4 How does Stewart's attitude to the fête change?

5 Why do Gosforth and Milly try to carry on with preparations for the fête?

6 What are the functions of the characters of a) the Vicar and b) Mrs Pearce in this play?

7 When the fête is over, Gosforth and Milly intend to 'sort it out'. Script this conversation, including Stewart if you wish. What will be said, and how will it be said?

A Talk in the Park

1 Choose one of the characters. Explain the background to what drives them to talk to their listener, referring to the text as appropriate.

2 Choose one of the characters. Explain why they respond as they do when spoken to by one of the other characters.

General

1 How well do we get to know the characters in the individual plays? What are the strengths and limitations of the characters within their one-act plays?

2 Choose one of the characters from one of the plays. In presenting the character to an audience, what aspects of the character would you choose to highlight? How might they be conveyed successfully to an audience?

3 What are Ayckbourn's intentions in presenting these characters to the audience/reader? How successful is he in creating these characters and in achieving his intentions?

B Themes

1 What are the *Confusions* of the title? How are the characters affected by their confusion?

2 How many failed relationships are presented in the play as a whole? What reasons are there for the failure of these relationships?

3 Choose one of the plays and examine the relationships portrayed in it. Which characters are most at fault? Why? Does Ayckbourn want us to take sides?

4 What does Ayckbourn want us to think of the characters in his plays? Should we laugh at them (or with them)?

5 Why does Ayckbourn use comedy as his medium? What effect does the comic treatment of a serious theme have upon the audience/reader?

6 'Might as well talk to yourself'. What were Alan Ayckbourn's intentions in writing the play? How successfully has he realised those intentions?

C In Performance

1 Select one of the plays. Draw up a design brief for that play. What set, furniture or props would be required? Consider the costumes for the characters: how might they suggest character? How might you design the set to allow its place to be taken quickly by the set for the next play? Where necessary, use evidence from the text to justify your decisions.

2 Select one of the plays. What are the themes particular

to that play? How, as a director, would you successfully draw the audience's attention to those themes? Consider character action and interaction.

3 Consider *Confusions* as a whole. What considerations would you need to make when preparing a design brief for all five plays? Consider sets, characters and costumes.

4 Select one of the characters from *Confusions*. What aspects of his/her character would you highlight in performance for the benefit of an audience? How? Why?

5 What reactions does Ayckbourn intend the audience/reader to have to the content of *Confusions*? How does he set about achieving them? Would he be successful in achieving the reaction he intends?

6 'Ayckbourn gives theatre-goers a good night out. But he also leaves them asking themselves "Are we really like that?"' (Michael Billington). Would *Confusions* provide you with a good night out? What would you take from it at the end of a performance?

D Criticism

1 What are the strengths and weaknesses of the one-act play form? Why do you think Ayckbourn chose to use one-act plays for *Confusions*?

2 Ayckbourn is concerned in *Confusions* with 'separation, obsession and isolation'. How does he make these themes acceptable to an audience/reader? How successful is he in doing so?

3 Ayckbourn has said that the most rewarding form of laughter is that which arises from an audience which understands and recognises the characters it sees onstage. How might an audience of *Confusions* identify with the characters?

4   Ayckbourn 'is at his most serious when he is at his
    funniest'. (Michael Billington). Do you agree? What
    does he hope to achieve through his comedy? Why,
    indeed, does he choose comedy as his medium?

BIBLIOGRAPHY

Specific attention is paid to *Confusions* in
Michael Billington, *Alan Ayckbourn* (Macmillan, 1983)
Oleg Kerensky, *The New British Drama* (Hamish
Hamilton, 1977)
Malcolm Page, (ed.) *File on Ayckbourn* (Methuen, 1989)

The best introduction to Ayckbourn's work and his
attitudes to it is
Ian Watson (ed.), *Conversations with Ayckbourn*
(Macdonald, 1981; Faber, 1988)

Further works which feature Ayckbourn and may be of
interest are
Judith Cook *Director's Theatre* (Hodder and Stoughton,
1989)
John Russell Brown, *A Short Guide to Modern British
Drama* (Heinemann Educational Books, 1982)
Benedict Nightingale, *An Introduction to 50 Modern British
Plays* (Pan, 1982)

In addition, the following Ayckbourn's full-length plays are
of value:
Three Plays (*Absurd Person Singular, Absent Friends, Bedroom
Farce*) (Penguin)
The Norman Conquests (Penguin)
Joking Apart and Other Plays (also contains *Ten Times Table,
Just Between Ourselves* and *Sisterly Feelings*) (Penguin)
A Chorus of Disapproval (Faber)
A Small Family Business (Faber)
Woman in Mind (Faber)
Henceforward . . . (Faber)

APPENDIX

The Major Plays of Alan Ayckbourn

Mr Whatnot	Stoke-on-Trent 1963; London 1964.
Relatively Speaking	Scarborough 1965; London 1967.
How the Other Half Loves	Scarborough 1969; London 1970.
Time and Time Again	Scarborough 1971; London 1972. (ITV 1976)
Absurd Person Singular	Scarborough 1972; London 1973. (BBC 1985)
The Norman Conquests	Scarborough 1973; London 1974. (ITV 1977)
Absent Friends	Scarborough 1974; London 1975. (BBC 1985)
Confusions	Scarborough 1974; London 1976.
Bedroom Farce	Scarborough 1975; London 1977. (ITV 1980)
Just Between Ourselves	Scarborough 1976; London 1977. (ITV 1978)
Ten Times Table	Scarborough 1977; London 1978.
Joking Apart	Scarborough 1978; London 1979.
Sisterly Feelings	Scarborough 1978; London 1980.
Taking Steps	Scarborough 1979; London 1980.
Season's Greetings	Scarborough 1980; London 1982. (BBC 1986)

Way Upstream	Scarborough 1981; London 1982. (BBC 1988)
Intimate Exchanges	Scarborough 1982; London 1984.
A Chorus of Disapproval	Scarborough 1984; London 1985. (Filmed 1989)
Woman in Mind	Scarborough 1985; London 1986.
A Small Family Business	London 1987.
Henceforward . . .	Scarborough 1987; London 1988.
Man of the Moment	Scarborough 1988.
The Revengers' Comedies	Scarborough 1989.